WE_____

Writing the Art Monster

Caroline Hagood

SPUYTEN DUYVIL
New York City

Library of Congress Cataloging-in-Publication Data

Names: Hagood, Caroline, author.
Title: Weird girls : writing the art monster / Caroline Hagood.
Description: New York City : Spuyten Duyvil, [2022]
Identifiers: LCCN 2022027685 | ISBN 9781956005776 (paperback)
Subjects: LCGFT: Essays.
Classification: LCC PS3608.A378 W45 2022 | DDC 814/.6--dc23/eng/20220622
LC record available at https://lccn.loc.gov/2022027685

For all the women who have been told they were too much.

*"I love weird girls. I am a weird girl.
I've always been a weird girl."*
—Jill Soloway

1

I slept with my childhood diary under my pillow: pink, self-serious, full of wild hope in my own words, with a huge lock on it—keep out world, but also break in. When I wrote in my diary about how the Wicked Witch of the West was a writer, I put her words in red because otherwise I couldn't tell them from my own. I told the world, *surrender,* but it never did.

I marvel that even so early in my little life I had streaked my page, that white, supposedly innocent land, with blood. It seems I'd caught myself being monstrous again. I didn't even intend it. It just happened, and I was helpless to hinder it. As Helene Cixous puts it, "Who, surprised and horrified by the fantastic tumult of her drives...hasn't accused herself of being a monster? Who, feeling a funny desire stirring inside her (to sing, to write, to dare to speak, in short, to bring out something new), hasn't thought she was sick?"

My obsession with the female monster was catalyzed by witnessing the Wicked Witch of the West in *The Wizard of Oz* one fateful evening. See, people use the word fateful without really meditating on its life story. The fates of Greek mythology, for instance—Clotho who spins, Lachesis who measures, and Atropos who cuts; her name meaning something like unturnable, representing, no doubt, the inevitability of death and maybe even life itself. Shakespeare later echoed these fates in his three witches, the weird sisters of *Macbeth,* just boiling boiling toil and trouble all through the night. Which is the long way of saying, in its folds fate holds all women with the power to predict something wicked this way comes.

2

Like many weird kids, I didn't have television growing up. But we did have movies to insert into the ancient VCR. One of them was *The Wizard of Oz*. Even then I saw the need for a woman-made mythology, a man's world rewritten by women, a wizard's world rewritten by witches. Most importantly, I saw that the Wicked Witch of the West was a writer, which is what I wanted to be more than anything. As Virginia Woolf knew, "When, however, one reads of a witch being ducked, of a woman possessed by devils, of a wise woman selling herbs...we are on the track of a lost novelist, a suppressed poet, of some mute and inglorious Jane Austen, some Emily Bronte who dashed her brains out on the moor or mopped and mowed about the highways crazed with the torture that her gift had put her to."

In the movie, above Emerald City the witch writes in black smoke with her broomstick, *surrender Dorothy*. When I read the book, I found that the Witch of the North, too, was a scribe: "She took off her cap and balanced the point on the end of her nose, while she counted 'One, two, three' in a solemn voice. At once the cap changed to a slate, on which was written in big, white chalk marks: 'LET DOROTHY GO TO THE CITY OF EMERALDS.'" In this moment, I started seeing a connection between women, monsters, and creativity, and later I would add mothers to the mix.

In a *Washington Post* interview, Yoko Ono weighs in on the celebration of wizards and the degradation of witches: "Very interestingly, if you said, 'Yes, I'm a wizard' or 'You're a wizard,' that's a compliment. A wizard is a male version of a witch. Why is it bad when it's women? Because then immediately you want to burn them."

3

Years later, when I read Elizabeth Wurtzel's *Bitch: In Praise of Difficult Women*, I realized "bitch" was another word for "witch: in our society. Wurtzel herself angers people and has been called everything, including the title of her aforementioned book. Despite, or maybe because of, those accusations, when I read her writing, my brain valve switches on, and that's all I care about. The real performance of Wurtzel's piece is this: she embodies the brilliant but difficult women she describes, even as she traces the etiology of her own fascination.

As a reader, I was not so much watching her tell as watching her. Her writing drips with all the indicators of the female subversion she describes, the trappings of the femme fatale (also known as "vamp" from vampire), the beauty that maims. I write in praise of Wurtzel's erudition on the subject of "difficult" women writers, of witches and bitches, even if we are both a pain in your posterior, and perhaps because of it. As you're reading this, beware, because maybe my writing also holds a cloak beneath a comma, a dagger behind every sentence.

John Updike, who wrote *The Witches of Eastwick*, says, "What interests me is why men think of women as witches. It's because they're so fascinating and exasperating, so other." It only occurred to me in adulthood that not only are all the people of Oz perhaps parts of Dorothy, but also, maybe most of all, the witches. It's easier to project the bedeviling parts of women onto witches. At the end of the day, a wart-nosed old hag mounting a broomstick, screwing the devil, and shooting fireballs is far less frightening than your complex, layered, unknowable wife.

4

Then there's the historical feminist underpinnings of Oz's enchantress. One inspiration for L. Frank Baum's 1900 book *The Wonderful Wizard of Oz* was his mother-in-law, women's rights activist Matilda Joslyn Gage. In her 1893 book *Woman, Church and State*, Gage wrote about how with the religious belief system that gave man God-sanctioned power over the supposedly weaker and more sinful women came the saying, "one wizard to 10,000 witches," and thus the witch hunt became mostly about women. We see women's expected ancillary role from the beginning of Baum's book when we discover that "Dorothy lived in the midst of the great Kansas prairies, with Uncle Henry, who was a farmer, and Aunt Em, who was the farmer's wife." But the witch didn't have to be any farmer's wife. That's the thing.

The night I watched *The Wizard of Oz* was fateful because it inaugurated my fascination with this green-faced, tale weaving female monster. She seemed to hold inside her a constellation of things about being a woman and being a writer, something to do with my deep dark desires and the almost sexual excitement I got when I wrote.

And what of my own inner monster? I love and fear her, I hide her and show her off. Even the mention of her sends a thrill through me. But I'm scared to tell you too much about her even now. It seems risky to let you too near. Like all monsters, her survival has depended on the distance I've given her from the pitchfork-wielding villagers. She started as a monster infant, but now she's an adult and her tenure here has become problematic. She's ripping me to shreds, requesting room service, hookers, cigars. What frightens and excites me most, though, is I've gotten to a point where everything I write is tattooed with her escape attempts.

5

In the movie, Dorothy's description of her first witch spotting is pretty wonderful in its upheaval of the natural order of things—the way the film's world is remade by her arrival in it. She sings the story to the Munchkins, again recalling a writer recounting a narrative: "What happened was just this: The wind began to switch—the house to pitch. And suddenly the hinges started to unhitch. Just then, the witch—to satisfy an itch—went flying on her broomstick thumbing for a hitch." Whoa and the sexual innuendo. I never saw that as a kid.

When Dorothy takes the dead witch's broom to the wizard, it's all neatly tied up as opposed to the wild way it used to be when the witch wielded it—as though Medusa were returned with her lovely hair snakes flat-ironed, so that she murders no more men through that maddening stiffening of horror and desire.

It almost seems that the very presence of the witch causes the house to undo and reconstruct itself in her image. It reminds me of two houses that obsess me: the home that becomes a labyrinth overnight in Mark Danielewski's novel *House of Leaves*, and the unusual angles of the house in Shirley Jackson's *The Haunting of Hill House*. What's so apt is that Jackson (who called herself a witch on various occasions) writes this famous haunted house novel but also pens books about domestic life and childrearing that she aptly titles *Life Among the Savages* and *Raising Demons*. Which means what, exactly? The real haunted house is the family home.

6

Don't forget that Dorothy's mistaken (if it's actually a mistake) for a witch multiple times too, so it's like she's destroying herself, her own female power, when she melts the Wicked Witch. Nevertheless, she becomes a witch slayer. Serial killer, really. She kills not one but two witches. It all begins when she crushes the Wicked Witch of the East with her cyclone-spun home. After this little debacle, the Winkies rejoice. In the movie, this all culminates in the orgiastic crescendo of an ensemble piece, the grotesquely chipper *Ding Dong the Witch is Dead.*

There couldn't be a more gleeful celebration of the vanquishing of threatening female might than the one that follows that little slaughter. Just to comfort us that the witch won't be popping back up and that she's gone to the correct place, we are reassured repeatedly that she's in hell: "She's gone where the Goblins go / Below…Below… Below Yo — ho, let's open up and sing / And ring the bells out. / Ding Dong! The merry-oh! / Sing it high Sing it… low / Let them know / The Wicked Witch is dead!" Talk about exorcising the witch to purify the culture. I picture her roaming around with Orpheus, in the Cocteau movie, also capable of eavesdropping on radio messages from the dead, after going through the mirror and attaining the underworld. But that's just me.

7

T hen *The Wizard of Oz* delves deeper into institutional-ized patriarchy when "Three Heralds, the Mayor, the Barrister, the Coroner, and the City Fathers" (and this is straight from the screenplay) approach Dorothy. Yes, the "City Fathers." The mayor says, "I welcome you most regal-ly," but the barrister gets down to business by bringing us back to the nitty-gritty matter of categorizing the witch's corpse: "But we've got to verify it legally that the witch is," and they all chime in on different parts of this one, "mor-ally, ethic'ly, Spiritually, physically, / Positively, absolutely, / Undeniably and reliably Dead!"

Next, the Mayor declares it "a day of Independence For all the Munchkins and their descendants!" This all has particular significance since, in addition to the free labor of slaves and the elimination of the native population, America was built on witch anxiety, as in the case of the Salem witch trials. Thus the singers have all neatly glossed in a single, sick, and chipper David Lynch-worthy ditty America's formation and foibles: a nation built on crushed bodies—and particularly those of women and people of color. Ding-Dong, the Genocide.

8

My mother, too, has her witchy side. Don't worry, she won't be offended. She embraces it, and this is just part of what makes her intriguing. I mostly mean she's spicy, and maybe a bit testy when pushed to the brink. But she also has a special spark that other mothers don't have. She shines like something sharp, is perilous and stunning. She told me at a young age that if a little boy ever treated me badly I should "pop him in the snout." I didn't ever do this, but the license she'd given me—to protect and value myself—lived inside me ever after. It didn't stop me from being frequently uncertain of myself, but I felt its presence, just like I felt her presence, everywhere I went, no matter what I was doing. I still do. Maybe we have always been monster women. She reminds me of the heroine of a Western, *Annie Get Your Gun*. I half expect her to stalk into my bar, pistol cocked and demand a duel at sun-up. Those spurs of hers are sharp.

I recently discovered, with little surprise, that my mom—this fiercely loving woman who can be a bit on the wicked witch side if you catch her at the wrong moment—had played the witch in a 2nd grade *Hansel and Gretel* production. Apparently, she forgot her one line, which was, "help!", knocked down all the trees in the fake forest, and now declares it to have been both her "stage debut" and her "finale."

9

I have always felt some deep sense of creativity and power to be found in monsters, ghosts, ghouls, witches, haunted houses, in learning to dwell in darkness without reaching after light. The architecture of my creative life was always built like Hill House, the angles all somewhat off. But there's something greater to be gained by tilting your head to take them in. At night when we drove in the car, I squinted my eyes, and the taillights became evil fairy things. As all the adults who visited our house reminded me, I was such a "sweet girl," but there appeared to be some sort of nascent insurrection inside of me.

Maybe it all started with the *Frankenstein* epiphany I had in the art corner my mom made me. This was well before I knew the word epiphany, back when I was just starting to embrace any flicker of creative power. In that art corner, I first turned off parts of my mind and body so I could turn on others. I decided to do anything in the service of writing great books. I sat there, at the age of ten and wrote my first novel, with pencil in a Marble composition notebook. It was called *A Light in Darkness* and it was about the boy I knew who was adopted by his aunt and uncle because his mother was a drug-addict. My magnum opus was abysmal of course, but it was a start. It was the beginning of this monster project in a sense, not that I could have known it then.

I had recently seen and read *Frankenstein* for the first time. I remember sitting at that desk and staring at my hand until I went into a kind of trance, thinking how easily it could be taken apart, but also of all the radically new things that could be made from its disparate parts. I felt this to be a metaphor for how I saw creativity and writing in particular. This was my first realization that "reality," "time," "space," "knowledge," and all those good things we learned about in school weren't set in stone but more like floating islands. They could all be rearranged, remade. Then I wrote from this Frankenstein-inflected mental space. It was my call to adventure. I stayed in that trance, typing until my fingers felt they might melt off, but in a good way, practically praying to Mary Shelley to bring on the language.

10

I remember the day I traded my sweat suits for "woman clothes" that I wore like a costume. As a child I studied females like a feral Harriet the Spy. I collected the pieces and sewed them together into a feminine amalgam that was going to be me. Building myself was like being Dr. Frankenstein and creating a monster. Why was the creation of a female self so much more a language of fragments?

I will always remember the day I painted my nails siren red and rode my bike as fast as I could, shouting the words I was writing as I rode, feeling the full electric shock of my own creativity. I contained whole countries of potency and story. I pedaled faster and faster until time and space were chopped in half. Did I scare myself a little? Yes. But I stayed in this moment because this was, counterintuitive as it may seem, my happy place.

Years later at a writing conference, I told a lovely clever woman—because all women who change your life are lovely and clever—about that childhood bike ride. I asked her what I should do about the fact that I had all these "monster things" I wanted to write about that I absolutely didn't feel I could confess to publicly. She told me to write a secret book, which led me here. But the scary yet thrilling thing is that now you are reading it.

11

When I called my mom to tell her my second poetry book was going to be published, she said, "well are you working on your next book? Keep on chugging." As an example of the non-relaxing advice on relaxing my mother espouses, see this quote by Michael Caine she emailed me in the middle of the night: "Be like a duck. Calm on the surface, but always paddling like the dickens underneath." But some days I just wanted to be calm underneath. Growing up, I couldn't decide whether I resented her for making me an anxiety case or worshipped her for making me a hard-working writer. I am still recovering from my mother's attempts to build a child prodigy.

Granted, she meant well. She was trying to give me all she was never given, but it was a lot of pressure to try to live up to her expectations. At the same time, she carefully recorded the "songs" I told her. She saw them for what they were: early poems. I've never told her I initially felt safe in poetry because I was dyslexic, and nobody could tell me I was getting the grammar wrong. She called me a writer even then. And this meant everything.

Recently I discovered on a late-night Internet romp that there's this trend where women are making their fingers look like candy canes, complete with the hook, so they resemble a witch's crooked finger. I feel, as with all horror items, drawn to these sweet peppermint atrocities, and repelled. The night I finished writing *A Light in Darkness*, I read Anne Sexton's "Her Kind" for the first time: "I have gone out, a possessed witch, / haunting the black air, braver at night; / dreaming evil, I have done my hitch / over the plain houses, light by light: / lonely thing, twelve-fingered, out of mind. / A woman like that is not a woman, quite. / I have been her kind."

I couldn't stop talking about the poem with my parents that evening. If they'd been a different sort, they might have contacted the police at that point, but they knew the mythos I'd grown up on. They were aware that I was an only child, but my real siblings were lady monsters from books and movies. What's more, I could have sworn I recognized Sexton's "hitch" in her witchy description from that catchy witch-slaying tune in *The Wizard of Oz,* and its magic woman who "went flying on her broomstick thumbing for a hitch." Had Anne Sexton and I been salivating over that same green-faced marvel? The guy who wrote *Wicked* certainly had.

12

And so, as a small thing, long before I had a term for it, I'd taken a holy vow to become an "art monster," like Jenny Offill writes about in her 2014 novel *Dept of Speculation*. I can't remember the last time I got coffee with a woman and/or mother who was also an artist/writer where the art monster didn't come up implicitly or explicitly. There has been a fascinating debate going on surrounding this notion that I've been following compulsively.

The concept probably dates back to the very first creative person, and certainly to the first woman who tried to make cave art while bouncing a baby. But the current conversation derives from Offill's book, wherein this woman vows to remain husband-free, a marvelous shimmering creator rather than created, which women so rarely get to be. Offill writes, "My plan was to never get married. I was going to be an art monster instead. Women almost never become art monsters because art monsters only concern themselves with art, never mundane things. Nabokov didn't even fold his umbrella. Véra licked his stamps for him."

With Offill in mind, Claire Dederer comes out with a much-discussed *Paris Review* piece on what's to be done with the work of monstrous men. As you read on, it deepens into an essay on how women writers must, on some level, become monstrous to make their art. To clarify, Dederer refers to the supposed "monstrousness" of a woman taking time for her typing, away from husband and children and her perceived duties as eternal caretaker, not the monstrousness of, say, offing someone to find writing time.

13

But the woman in Offill's novel struggles to be the art monster because she does get married and have children. The book therefore plays on the notion of domesticity and artistry as being mutually exclusive—a notion I want to shoot down, even though I completely understand the struggle to which it refers. In fact, this is exactly why I need to shoot it down—because that struggle is so real. Yet *Dept. of Speculation* secretly knows better. The book may be about a woman whose art suffers because of the vagaries of "womanhood," but it's written by one whose art most certainly doesn't: because she has written *Dept of Speculation*.

Offill makes this art monster comment in her novel and women writers seize on it, and the question is: why, what are they seizing on, and what is the history of this seizing? Offill's character talks about how she was going to be an art monster—a distinctly male form, a writer who focuses only on his art to the detriment of his family, but nobody minds because he's a man. But what if the art monster is a woman?

Dept of Speculation highlights some uncomfortable but widely held beliefs that being a mother/wife and an art monster are mutually exclusive, that an art monster is a man, that being someone obsessed with your art makes you a monster/bad person, and so forth. On the other hand, this mutual exclusivity is an illusion all along. "The wife" is a character who's prevented from writing by her mother/wife status, but Offill as real-life author has used this very material to make her art, the book *Dept of Speculation*.

So, what Offill has really done is write a book that dramatizes the challenge for women writers while simultaneously demonstrating the way they overcome it: by embracing their art monster status, grabbing it up along with the time and space to make their art, using the experience of being a woman/mother to fuel the writing if that happens to be their situation, and then writing that book, even as kids cascade from their body. At the same time, this is my only tweet that went even remotely viral, so you can see the challenges of trying to be a writer while adorned in children: "Everyone in the writing world: attend as many writing residencies as possible Me: (with two kids dangling from my body) How?"

14

As Offill frames it, 1) if women try to snatch their own time and space to make their art they are treated as monsters; 2) it's hard to take this time because of the "mundane," as she calls them, "duties" of domestic life that threaten to eat these women whole; 3) but since they must take this time to make their art, and since this means they will be treated as monsters, why not embrace it? Why not find creative possibility in that role of art monster? And so, Offill writes, "The wife has begun planning a secret life. In it, she is an art monster. She puts on yoga pants and says she is going to yoga, then pulls off onto a country lane and writes in tiny, cramped handwriting on a grocery list." "The Wife" becomes the "Art Monster." An upgrade, I'd say. Not just Rilke and Coleridge (in the book), but she is the art monster, and it's not a loss but a win. She writes on the grocery list no less: rechristening this domestic document as a space of art making. She is not merely grocery shopper, mother, and "wife," but also writer, artist.

I want to reclaim monster, and particularly art monster as lesbians have done with the word "dyke." This embracing of a queer lens is relevant here since I believe that being the writer I need to be requires leaving any traditional understanding of gender at the door. So, I am taking back the monster from its negative associations and the way it has been wielded historically against women (the witch hunt, for example), and I'm taking back the art monster from men. I'm also taking it back for mothers. Brilliant as it is, *Dept of Speculation* is a book that truly wonders if mother and art monster can co-exist, and I'm here to tell you that they can—even if it's a bloody battle.

15

There's often a play with conventional notions of gender when it comes to female monsters, which provides
them with their ability to go beyond social boundaries
and be, essentially, transcendent. Jeffrey Jerome Cohen
writes in his *Monster Theory,* "the woman who oversteps
the boundaries of her gender role risks becoming a Scylla,
Weird Sister, Lilith." In Macbeth, Banquo tells the Weird
Sisters, "You should be women, / And yet your beards forbid
me to interpret / That you are so."

In the first folio edition, Shakespeare called these sisters,
"Posters of the Sea and Land," which makes me think again
of their not quite fitting into any one category and of my
love of mermaids. Marcela Sulak writes of how those who
didn't march within the conventional lines of gender used
to be viewed as having narrative and visionary powers:
"In various other cultures, hermaphrodites/androgynous/
intersex people were considered sacred and charged with
special tasks such as storytelling and prophesy."

There's a bliss to the monstrous freedom of gender play,
too. As Cohen puts it, nailing monster theory yet again,
"The habitations of the monsters...are more than dark
regions of uncertain danger: they are also realms of happy
fantasy, horizons of liberation. their Monsters serve as
secondary bodies through which the possibility of other
genders, other sexual practices, another social customs can
be explored. Hermaphrodites, Amazons, and lascivious
cannibals beckon from the edges of the world, the most

distant planets of the galaxy." Maybe this is all part of why, to think of myself as an art monster from an early age, I had to conceive of myself as something that lived beyond the boundaries of gender, or at least what was carved out for girls. As a "young lady," I'd been culturally conditioned against everything that a talented writer supposedly was.

16

Some days I can see backwards from a time of being a kid to suddenly copying my mother as she brushed her hair, thinking, finally, this, now this must be what it is to be a woman. When she asked me what I was doing, I told her I was learning. I'd made the first addition in a lifelong arithmetic of understanding what I was supposed to be that was different from what my father was—math with no solution. But as I watched my father shave, the little hairs running down the drain, I wondered why this wasn't my province, why I had to choose one or the other. And then when I got married and had kids, my gender role felt further cemented. Before me loomed a very *Brady Bunch* situation, a wavelength of bake sales and bento box lunches perfectly arranged. But no. Some wildness survived.

Perhaps the hardest thing about being a woman is watching the year repeat its days—each one falling into the gap between what I am when I first wake up and can't yet call up my whole story in the outside world, and what I become when I leave my house—a thing to be seen through a spy glass by all citizens of Gotham. I try to recall how a woman walks through endless streets and construction sites, what kind of armor I wore yesterday to evade the comments that would otherwise undo me. I wake up feeling somewhat good about myself until I'm instructed by some guy on the subway to, "choke on a dick," and then I must, let's say, regroup.

My early need to transcend the limitations of gender

sheds light on how the monster is tied to a sort of queering impulse. This could be why Susan McCabe writes of the monstrous femme fatale as a "beard for queer sexuality." Technically, I'm a "woman," yes, but in terms of the "gender" of myself as a writer, if being a woman meant not claiming my writerly territory, I decided in this one way not to be her—not that woman at least. Parents, let your kids send you their own gender reveal cakes when they're ready.

I figured not being considered a woman might save both my life and creativity. In the 2018 *Comedy Lineup*, Aisling Bea echoes this sentiment with a bit on how men are intimidated by funny women, while women are intimidated by the fact that men can kill them with their hands. She tells a story in which a man walks down a street at night, when suddenly a funny woman jumps out at him screaming, "Pull my finger," and he's so terrified he…kills her.

There has often been a violence to the male will to creativity, and it has often been pitted against women. Yopie Prins says of the structure of lyric poetry and its reading processes, "The projected fantasy of a female body and a feminine voice through linguistic scattering, grammatical dismemberment, rhetorical contradiction—as well as other forms of disjunction, hiatus, and ellipsis-suggests why Sappho became exemplary of lyric in its irreducibly textual embodiment, and exemplary of lyric reading as well, in its desire to hypothesize a living whole from dead letters."

Uncomfortable questions lurk beneath Prins' description of Sappho as the exemplum of lyric. Her commentary confronts us with problems of gender and even violence. The Frankenstein-like fantasy of a dismembered female corpse imagined as a living whole is a disturbing one. Dismemberment goes beyond fragmentation because it implies a purposeful, aggressive division, and this crime is committed against the body of the female in this case.

18

Prins' gendered account reflects one of the problems of lyric poetry—and writing in general. As Matthew Rowlinson writes, "the silenced characters are typically women," and he continues to muse on "the proliferation of women who are mute, dead or exist only as image in Victorian lyric." Alice Bolin has a smart book on how dead girls have fueled the television, book, and movie universe for as long as anyone can remember.

If gender is both a prison and a performance, I was tired of the restrictive theater in which I said sorry over and over until I died. At the same time, as Paul Theroux's description of being a man as wearing an ill-fitting coat shows, there's stuff wrong with being a man, too. So I didn't want to be a part of either camp when it came to writing. I just wanted to relate to my paper without any of that nonsense coming between us. But it's easier said than done.

Maybe all our minds are made of things more nuanced than either sugar and spice and everything nice or slugs and snails and puppy dog tales. Personally, I'm beginning to suspect my mind's composed of Bengal tigers and thickets of nightshade. I have always felt I needed to be prepared to lead a rebel army in a dystopian novel. Not that anybody would know this about me.

19

I seem pleasing (a huge part of the problem) and cheerful, and in many ways I am. I'm the textbook Brooklyn mother. But here's the thing: I need to stop being pleasant, a woman constructed for your pleasures. I need to talk filthy if I need to. I am here to take no prisoners, except for you; you're kind of cute. But, let's be honest, that won't happen. I have two kids. I go to "sing-alongs" and coffee shops when I get a "sitter."

I do more of the cooking, grind spices with mortar and pestle. I worry over every little thing for my kids even though they live the lives of emperors, and really the only thing they will suffer from is being too lucky. I procreate. That and lope around my house like an intruder, eating all the sweet things in the cupboard in a counterintuitive attempt to lose the baby weight, write, teach, vow to write the great American novel, but mostly just sit in a bean bag chair eating Flamin' Hot Cheetos.

I wonder if there's someone out there who can read the more difficult text of me, even as I put on this act of having normal feelings when I'm in public—like, *oh yeah, everything is fine, work has been tough, and can you believe this winter?* Now, take that weirdo and make her a mother, give her all the related bodily surprises and emotional ups and downs, and see what happens. I mean, it's like a weird science experiment gone awry. *Bill Nye the Science Guy* type of stuff.

20

What is it they say, though? It's the silent ones that are the most deadly? Except that I never shut up, and I think they were talking about farts, so maybe strike that one from the record. The point is, I've never understood why you can't be both literary luminary and loving caretaker, or just minimally not an asshole, both monster and mother. But I do get where the belief in the mutual exclusivity of these identities comes from. The mother occupies a strange position in the monster mythos, for sure. She's at once monstered and kept far away from all that is considered the territory of the male art monster.

One psychiatrist we read about in my theory class (or did I make this up?) thought people who hung themselves had mother issues due to the correlation he drew between umbilical cord and noose. As this association between loving link to mother and self-murder weapon indicates, the connection to dear mama is never an easy one. Perhaps this helps explain the prevalence of monstrous mothers in our media and mythology.

And so all the previous pages point to why, when I became a mother I felt the need to connect to my inner art monster with even more fervor. A play with gender suddenly more necessary than ever to circumvent just the issue Offill describes: the mother-woman trap when it comes to art and just generally asserting oneself as actor and not an acted upon in one's own life. It's honestly a territory I must try to carve out for myself. I don't have a clear-cut community since I don't identify with many of the books and general views on motherhood supposedly aimed at "people like me," so I need to find my own space. As you might guess, I never found my tribe at sing-along classes, though I was always looking.

21

I have found the experience of being a mother to be a wild one—starting with that searing nature of birth. I disagree with the idea that motherhood must domesticate you; it's also a feral experience that you can choose to keep and treat that way. In the end, I identify more with Maggie Nelson's exploration of the queerness of motherhood in *The Argonauts* than with any of the pastel-colored mommy books I've been given. I have also found becoming a mother to be something that feeds my art monster nature, and being an art monster something that feeds my mother nature, counter to much of the art monster narratives out there.

I mean that I don't find being a mother and being an art monster to be mutually exclusive, but I absolutely find it to be practically a fight to the death to ensure that the duties and expectations of "mother" and "woman" don't suck up the artist in me—or at least all the time I must make my art. I think if you fight tooth and nail for your art, being a mother can feed it.

Of course, this is all dependent on having the health and means necessary for basic functioning, and I'm sadly aware that this is not something to which everyone has equal access. The question, then, comes down to an old one that Virginia Woolf was exploring all those years ago in *A Room of One's Own*—carving out the physical and mental space to actually make the art that could conceivably be sparked by the extraordinary experience of parenthood. We need to help build those spaces for ourselves but also for others.

22

When we were both grown up, or college age at least, I saw the kid I'd written that first novel about. He was just out of rehab, and I'd not yet quit drinking but I should have. We went to the local casino near where we were staying in Puerto Rico. The night ended when he tried to trade me to a local for rum. I called my epic-loving, mythologically minded father to pick me up after the casino incident. He rolled up in front, and when I got in, he asked me whether I was ready to come home to Ithaka. I had never been so ready. I loved that I was posited as Odysseus in this speculative epic. Or was I Telemachus? Either one is fine, as long as I get to go out and have my adventure, and not be Penelope weaving, fending off suitors, weaving, waiting for her man to come home.

I'd always had literary epic aspirations foiled by each new review I read that said essentially women couldn't write genius works like men, that they were either sad girls or monsters—or both simultaneously—if they tried to write an ambitious book. I felt foiled each new time somebody like V.S. Naipaul claimed he didn't like women's writing, just another Norman Mailer turning his nose up at the sniffs he got from the "ink of the women," to prove that women were worse writers than men and perhaps even genetically incapable of writing at all.

I suspect there's a little of the heroic in us all, though. I just need to find mine. It's in there somewhere, cowering beneath all the Paw Patrol paraphernalia. But I hate that

I must fight off impostor syndrome to take up any space at all, especially when I remember what Mailer said about women writers, and how this belief is alive and well today. I also don't enjoy how before every writing appearance I must remind myself that I'm not a cartoon character impersonating a human adult writer woman.

23

With his offensive riff on the whiff of women's ink, Mailer takes us on a guided tour of all the ways creative women can be viewed as monstrous. In Mailer's large-scale takedown of women's talent, we see, not surprisingly, their ability twisted up with their supposedly repugnant sexuality—woman writer as potential prostitute, weird lesbian, or failed mother (possibly all depicted by Julia Roberts at one point or another).

The female monster as tied to both creativity and procreativity is as old as time, or at least can be traced to whenever women's stunning and sometimes gory reproductive capabilities got folded into a simultaneously frightening and awe-inspiring belief in her potential for creation, and its flip side, destruction, which all needed to be kept in check. Let's not forget that so many women accused of being witches were midwives and/or mothers themselves—or, another sin, too old to make children or be hot anymore.

What a woman's body can create, destroy, and emit—particularly when these creations and emissions are paired with the supposed mysteries of her psychological life—essentially form the basis of at least half the horror stories out there. When the memoirist Meghan Daum tells her students that if anyone's going to love their books, some must hate them, she says it inevitably encourages a breakthrough where they write about another belittled subject, their digestive tracks.

Maybe this isn't such a bad urge. I still find bathroom humor humorous and hope I always do. James Joyce can pull off a multi-page bathroom scene of incomparable beauty, complete with the warmth of recently generated waste, but so can you. I like to refer to my computer diary as "that whole Doogie Howser hot mess." So much of it (perhaps too much of it) has made its way in here.

24

With these creations and emissions in mind, I started to draw strange connections between women creating literature and women creating babies (and women using the bathroom? Let's leave that for another book). Someone who also really got this correspondence between book and baby was the poet Hilda Doolittle, who described her books as 'still-born.' Even good old Yeats saw the correlation. In an introductory verse to *Responsibilities,* he wrote, "Although I have come close on forty-nine, / I have no child, I have nothing but a book."

Adrienne Rich knew all too well that we needed a radical reinterpretation of motherhood that connected the reproductive with the productive. I have started seeing so many parallels between biological and literary creation that I now see my writing as sex followed by popping a baby out on a medical table. As you can see, being me is the best and worst sex I've ever had.

25

The kind of writing that calls out to me in the night, and which I consider monstrous, also tends to be hybrid (in both form and content), a literary breed of monstrosity, sewn together from the bodies of different genres, a Frankenstein. See: every book Claudia Rankine has ever written. Just go out and buy them all right now. Rankine subtitles her book *Citizen*—which draws on techniques of poetry, memoir, and criticism, even including scripts for situation videos in its hybrid pages—"An American Lyric."

In *Incubation: A Space for Monsters,* Bhanu Kapil writes an ode to just the sort of monstrous creativity I worship. For me, finding it was like meeting my "vanishing twin," or the twin that gets absorbed into the other, except that we both clearly made it out of the womb, and we're not related. So, I'll just say locating Kapil's book was like finding a mind that could knock back against a wall I thought I was knocking at alone. Please also read her book.

Leslie Jamison calls her mix of literary criticism, memoir, and cultural criticism, in *The Recovering,* for one, speculative autobiography, an effort to map out what her creativity could look like. I'd like to make a motion to add this to the list of terms, like Maggie Nelson's auto-theory (although she wasn't the first to use this term), for some of the hybrid and super cool work being done by women writers today. Works like Kate Zambreno's *Heroines* and Maggie Nelson's *The Argonauts,* as well as Rankine's and Kapil's work (and the work of so many others—email me and I'll send you too long of a list), bring the personal into ingenious dialogue with the theoretical and political.

Basically: in my art monster quest, I became increasingly intrigued by writing that pushed the boundaries of what writing could be. Not surprisingly, the innovative results of this bloody writing—these composite creatures—cause critics to send many of these books (especially when written by women, and especially especially when written by women of color) to bed without supper for being supposedly wounded and self-focused.

What I think of as sad girl syndrome taints the analysis of these women's work—the tendency to portray the woman-identifying writer as a pathetic mope, guilty of the crime of thinking her mournful tale worthy of being told. In the end, for women writers, it often comes down to a choice between being portrayed as victim or perpetrator, as sad girl or monster—especially when you're a poet—and often both at once.

One such wonderful composite creature, Mary-Kim Arnold's *Litany for the Long Moment*, plays on this reductive take on women's personal writing as the terrain of "sad girls" in much the same way Chris Kraus did in *I Love Dick* when she defined her project as "Lonely Girl Phenomenology." In her introduction to *Litany for the Long Moment*, Carla Harryman writes that Arnold draws on the work of various artists "to fabricate a sagacious community of informant 'sad girls.'" As Zambreno puts it in *Heroines,* "the self-portrait, as written by a woman, is read as somehow dangerous and indulgent . . . indulging in the self as contrary to art."

Yet these women writers are not only continuing to write their personal experience, but they are doing so not against but in the very service of art. Far from self-indulgent, this layered work brings the strengths of both the public and private realms—what I like to think of as the close-up and long shot—to bear on the subject matter, ultimately allowing these writers to take a more comprehensive look at themselves but also at art and society at large.

Throughout *The Recovering*, Leslie Jamison strives to balance the imperatives of telling her own stories and telling the stories of other addicts. As a now-sober former addict, I appreciated both threads. Jamison tries to honor the AA doctrine of making it all about something larger than herself, and often portrays herself as trying to atone for being too self-absorbed. But I wonder if she would have had to take herself to task for her desire to talk about her own experience quite so much if she were one of those Drunk Male Geniuses she writes about.

That said, Jamison's personal narrative grows increasingly nuanced as it becomes braided with cultural and literary criticism and all these pieces of other people's lives. At a certain point in the book, she writes about her relief at finally spotting the mice she suspected she had in her house all along. I see this strange scene as a symbol of the work she does in *The Recovering*. The surfacing mice moment dramatizes the tension between her desire to think inwardly (often unfairly categorized as the action of a self-absorbed, drunk, confessional writer) or outwardly (categorized as the helpful, sober, writer of socially conscious prose), and the instant in which they come together to make this book—the mouse poised between inner tunnel and outer room. Jamison's stunning "speculative autobiography" allows us to encounter her subterranean animal right at the moment it pops its head out, made luminously visible by her writing.

26

And yet, as I became more intrigued by women's writing and read more and more criticism on it, it bothered me that all female stories are treated as wound showing. Chris Kraus writes of her treatment of emotion "as discipline, as form," rather than as an uncritical feeling dump.

In her book that uses techniques of fiction and memoir, among many others to brilliantly excavate female experience, *I Love Dick,* Kraus writes of the female monster, too:

"I explained to Warren about the difference between male and female monsters. 'Female monsters take things as personally as they really are. They study facts. Even if rejection makes them feel like the girl who's not invited to the party, they have to understand the reason why.' Monstrosity: the self as a machine. The Blob, mindlessly swallowing and engorging, rolling down the supermarket aisle absorbing pancake mix and jello and everyone in town. Unwise and unstoppable. The horror of The Blob is a horror of the fearless. To become The Blob requires a certain force of will. Every question, once it's formulated, is a paradigm, contains its own internal truth. We have to stop diverting ourselves with false questions. And I told Warren: I aim to be a female monster too."

Kraus didn't fit in the tiny body of any one genre, and I hope this can help me understand my own quest to create a new genre or technology for talking about women's experience. In addition to identifying the monstrous as the horse that breaks down the stall of definition (I paraphrase wildly here), Jack Halberstam calls the Gothic form a technology. I like that. I plan on awaiting a stormy night and then crafting a new genre for women in my "workshop of filthy creation," just like the one Dr. Frankenstein had. In the meantime, I'll make do with this sticky desk in my kids' room.

27

As I read Leslie Jamison on Kraus' use of parataxis in *I Love Dick*, I stopped over at Wikipedia to help me recall what the devil that was again. I discovered that Aileen Wuornos's (the serial killer portrayed by Charlize Theron in the movie, *Monster)* last words were an instance of parataxis. Now, I'm going to do the thing I tell my students never to do and quote Wikipedia in (formal?) writing: Parataxis is "used to describe a technique in poetry in which two images or fragments, usually starkly dissimilar images or fragments, are juxtaposed without a clear connection. Readers are then left to make their own connections implied by the paratactic syntax." Wuornos was executed on October 9, 2002, and her last words were: "Yes, I would just like to say I'm sailing with the rock, and I'll be back, like Independence Day, with Jesus. June 6, like the movie. Big mother ship and all, I'll be back, I'll be back." Wuornos doesn't feel the need to write in the connective tissue here. If you want to thread the words together, you have to complete this act in your own mind. In this way, her words meld with your own mind matter as you seek to sew them into anything that resembles articulation. Have fun with that.

I have read essay after essay denouncing women's writing as mere pain narratives. I concluded recently that every single review of a woman's writing (not just poetry) since Plath forms its judgments by whether the reviewer imagines the writer loves Plath. For an example of what I'm talking about, check out Jessa Crispin's *Boston Review* article on what she dubs wounded women writers, in which she touches on Leslie Jamison and Kate Zambreno, among others. She doesn't mention Plath explicitly, but both Zambreno and Jamison address her in their work, and Jamison loves her, so you see where I'm going with this. Crispin writes, "Suddenly women writers were being valued for their stories of surviving violence and trauma. Bestsellers such as Leslie Jamison's *The Empathy Exams* portrayed women as inherently vulnerable. The *New York Times Book Review* recently proclaimed 'a moment' for the female personal essayist." Let's just say, for reasons I've already articulated and will reveal more about later (stay tuned, wink wink), I didn't love seeing this portrayed as a bad thing.

Then, just as quickly, the female personal essay's moment was supposedly over. A *New Yorker* article declared the death of the personal essay, but I won't be attending the funeral. The article's author, Jia Tolentino, identifies personal writing with women and specifically with the kind of women's writing that makes people uncomfortable because it's too "personal," or what Tolentino refers to as "lost-tampon essays." Tolentino herself writes excellent personal essays, so I'm thinking she maybe just internalized the bad press women get for doing so? For writing what Plath and other women were labeled (negatively) as "confessional" or "sad girls" for doing.

Let's just say that I will continue to consume— voraciously, religiously, like I'm saving my own goddamn life—"lost-tampon essays" for as long as I live. As Kraus, writes in *I Love Dick*, "I think the sheer fact of women talking, being paradoxical, inexplicable, flip, self-destructive but above all else public is the most revolutionary thing in the world." And I would have to agree.

Dear women out there writing of your mesmerizing inner lands (where that lost tampon may be wandering still), I want to read everything you write. Please send it to me. The poet H.D. wrote *Helen in Egypt,* which reimagined the Trojan war from a female perspective, but we need more female epics. Let's do this.

I want to go on my hero's journey but I'm a woman, so would it have to be, like, a heroine's journey? But all we get is that shoddy feminine version which is whinier, requires identification with the masculine, and doesn't sound like half as much fun. Melissa Febos covered this beautifully and so much more in her intrepid *Girlhood* (or was it *Body Work*? Never mind, read them both). Of all the people who ever wanted to, what percentage of them got to write that great work? Got to populate the canon, make the literary-intellectual trains run on time? And how many women? How many women of color? How many trans women? How many queer women? You get my point.

But as I ponder the beginning of my projected epic, shit just keeps blowing up in my face, literally. Of dramatic plot, Aristotle wrote in his *Poetics,* "Well-constructed plots must neither begin nor end at haphazard points." But then my son comes bursting out of his room to inform me that my daughter has "exploded a poop bomb" in her diaper. So I ask my Muse, "Can I even write an epic when I have so many asses to wipe?" and she says, "Absolutely, your epic will be the better for it." But I was talking to myself all along, of course, so I'm not sure if that really counts.

And, unfortunately, anything I write will probably be treated as the output of a Mad Woman in the Attic, anyway. Kate Zambreno's *Heroines* looks at the ways in which women writers are cast, in contrast to their myth-making male counterparts, as mentally ill muses, mad women in the attic. In many ways the whole history of women's literature to date has been a question of how to free that woman from that theoretical attic.

30

Luckily, Carmen Maria Machado's *Her Body and Other Parties* brings the madwoman in the attic trope to the party. "The Husband Stitch" reanimates that girl with the ribbon around her neck that we used to whisper about at sleepovers. This girl is the perfect symbol for this particular story and for the collection as a whole. This ribbon, if undone, just might unleash the supposedly mad world that's always in danger of roaring out of all women should we be effectively opened.

In "The Resident," which takes place at a writing retreat, another female artist demands of our writer protagonist, "Do you ever worry...that you're the madwoman in the attic?...Do you ever worry about writing the madwoman-in-the-attic story?...You know. That old trope. Writing a story where the female protagonist is utterly batty. It's sort of tiresome and regressive and, well, done." Well, watch out, everyone, because that madwoman is roaring towards you at a velocity no ribbon or husband stitch can do a goddam thing about. As the narrator of "The Mothers," puts it, "something inside of me is breaking; I am a continent but I will not hold."

31

The textual madwoman in the attic is "mad" as in purportedly mentally ill, but also as in mad as hell and not going to take it anymore. This woman, with her rage and supposed lunacy all hidden away up there in the attic, is the ultimate female monster, isn't she? Like most ogres, we must see her from afar for her to remain so. This is the recursion of the monstrous: we don't want to look at the monster because we're afraid; we have only to look at the monster for her to become not monstrous at all; but it's the very act of not looking that seals the monstrous deal, leaving that woman eternally in the attic and eternally mad.

But Machado doesn't merely show us the madwoman in the attic; she unties that ribbon around her neck and takes us inside that madwoman's attic, into her mind and body, her interiority. We see what it feels like to be her. Even more striking, we often see that she is we. But by the time we feel this, that woman doesn't seem so very mad or so very monstrous after all. Because we are actually looking at her.

As the narrator of "The Mothers" tells us, "You never live with a woman, you live inside of her, I overheard my father say to my brother once." What her father refers to here is where at least some of the horror surrounding women and their interiority comes from—that uncanny sense of, "I came from her; I used to live inside her," that I have when I look at my own mother sometimes. (I'll spare you the other part of the father's equation here, the mandatory overdone castration anxiety stuff, the fear of the man's penis being lost to the dark continent of the woman's vagina sort of thing.)

32

If you think about it, though, there must be some sort of (unintentional) rejection of the maternal interiority, or we would never be born. Machado knows her theory and the intellectual traditions in which she trudges only too well, and she has fun with it. At one point in "The Resident," the writer character breaks out in sores and takes care of it by inserting "the pin into the original abjection."

But this is what all horror literature does—renders literal our internal ghoulies. Of abjection, Julia Kristeva writes, "There looms, within abjection, one of those violent, dark revolts of being, directed against a threat that seems to emanate from an exorbitant outside or inside, ejected beyond the scope of the possible, the tolerable, the thinkable." And this is precisely where I want reading to take me: "beyond the scope of the possible, the tolerable, the thinkable." Which leads me to Machado's particular innovation, her addition to the madwoman in the attic stuff, what I like to call her Abject-Mother-Baby-in-the-Basement literature.

In her story "Eight Bites," after getting bariatric surgery, our character finds a sobbing "body with nothing it needs: no stomach or bones or mouth. Just soft indents" in her basement. Curled, crying on the floor as the narrator starts kicking her (this creature comes from the weight she lost, so it's like kicking herself), it seems like a baby. But, later, after the character dies, she tells us that this woman creature comes to collect her in a maternal mode, to love her even though she wasn't loved back, and the narrator "will curl into her body, which was my body once."

Machado talks a lot about the mind, but she also clearly allows for a woman's body with its unthinking wants and needs and complaints and passions and ways backwards and forwards. All this talk of the body brings me to something else refreshing about her stories: yes, sex—ugly, beautiful, un-airbrushed intercourse; any collection that purports to hear the secret thoughts of porn stars is in a class all its own where coitus is concerned. "I pull him through the trees, and when we find a patch of clear ground. I shimmy off my pantyhose, and on my hands and knees offer myself up to him. I have heard all of the stories about girls like me, and I am unafraid to make more of them."

Machado certainly brings the body to the party, along with that tension and play between what lies outside the body and what lies within it. In "The Husband Stitch," after her husband does what we know he'll do all along and pulls the ribbon around her neck, the narrator notes, "If you are reading this story out loud, you may be wondering if that place my ribbon protected was wet with blood and openings, or smooth and neutered like the nexus between the legs of a doll."

Machado reviews and interviews carp on how she doesn't deal in in the "real," as when an interview in *The Atlantic* refers to her "refusal to adhere to the conventions of realism." To me this sounds like some sort of archaic madwoman in the attic lingo. Real according to whom? As for me, I adhere to Ambrose Bierce's definition of realism in his 1911 *Devil's Dictionary:* "Realism, n. The art of depicting nature as it is seen by toads."

In response to this discourse on the refusal of the real in her work, Machado responds, "In my work, I think non-realism can be a way to insist on something different. It's a way to tap into aspects of being a woman that can be surreal or somehow liminal—certain experiences that can feel, even, like horror."

In "The Resident," our writer "was reminded, for the umpteenth time, of Viktor Shklovsky's idea of defamiliarization; of zooming in so close to something, and observing it so slowly, that it begins to warp, and change, and acquire new meaning." This is also a great strategy for reading *Her Body and Other Parties*. The real strangeness in life is not the ghosts and monsters Machado conjures, but the appearance of our own body parts if we look at them up close for long enough, these outsides that accompany our insides, the part taken for the whole, the gazed upon everyday item that takes on the gravest characteristics of strangeness under sustained inquiry. Remarkably, this defamiliarization is also a tool. If we look at the supposedly normal, "real" structures of our lives as we looked at our now alien body parts, we might start to find them strange, to question them, to say, "wait a minute, why do we treat women's bodies quite like this?" We might even start to imagine new structures that could be made from all of it.

Forget Mars; the inside of a woman is the most gorgeous and frightening place in this whole universe in its anger, poignance, and possibility. The real terrain of Machado's collection, and my own, is the revelation that we humans are the real haunted houses, as we see in this book's initial stunning epigraph from Jacqui Germain: "My body is a haunted / house that I am lost in."

35

In Kate Zambreno's *Heroines,* she shares that she's always been trying to learn how to be a serious writer who writes important books. But this is hard to do when you're cast as the kooky muse or the mad woman in the attic again and again. Zambreno writes, "Days I worry, wonder—what if I'm not a writer? What if I'm a depressive masquerading as a notetaker? Is this the text of an author or a madwoman? It depends perhaps on who is reading it." I marvel, though, at a dazzling wordsmith like Zambreno feeling she must learn how to become a serious writer, or that, as Dederer says, to do this she may have to conceive of herself as a sort of monster.

The degree to which people get riled up by the concept of the art monster continues to fascinate me. Lauren Groff's tweet: "I just erased 2000 words on how much I hate the term 'art monster.' There's so much shrugging acceptance of mother-shaming in it. If your work is as important to you as your kids are, you're not a monster. You're an artist." Furthermore, Rebecca Solnit was not pleased with Dederer's art monster article, arguing essentially that writers need not be selfish people. But I don't think Dederer was saying that women must become bad people to make art. She was just saying that they need to snatch a certain degree of space and time, and they need to believe the work they're doing merits this. Astutely, Dederer stresses that when women do this, it's often coded as monstrous.

It's hard to get away from the terror that self-revelation is icky somehow, especially as a woman, that it reeks too much of the sad girl. Somehow the woman's self-portrait is treated with horror.

The problem is I'm obsessed with this sort of self-reference. Every time I meet anyone, I want to read their diary. And on my end, I want to write about this hand here with this hand, use this lurid and bifurcated mind to talk about this mind. Fernande Leger said he didn't know what a hand was until he saw it onscreen in the movies. Agnès Varda—in her magnificent essay film on the literal and figurative possibilities of gleaning, picking up trash or collecting mental tidbits, *The Gleaners and I* (*Les glaneurs et la glaneuse*)—shows us a close-up of her own wrinkled hand and says, "I mean this is my project: to film with one hand my other hand, to enter into the horror of it, I find it extraordinary." Put that in your pipe and smoke it. Yet I still wake with horror after sharing parts of myself in writing. But I still do it.

36

As for my own experience of finding magical art possibilities in trash as Varda had, when I was seven, my family visited a little island off the coast of Puerto Rico during hurricane season. The littered beaches resembled billowing garbage monsters with cans for eyes. I was in heaven. I understood the sorrow of hurricanes when the innkeeper's husband lightly touched her shoulder as she listed what she had lost in the storm, but I didn't understand that garbage—what people reject from "respectable society," as they often do with the monster, couldn't be exquisite—and I still don't.

I hatched a plan to build something out of the island's wreckage. I didn't have much to work with, so I went down to the ocean's edge and started sifting through the remnants. I imagined broken light bulbs to be functional, their light coming down in sprays to illuminate my work, and I told myself stories about the things I found. When I finally got my spoils back to the inn, I started building what I thought of as my trash monster sculpture. I wrapped broken Christmas ornaments in scraps of underwear, braided electrical wires and placed them atop my monument like fancy hairdos, and carved love letters into broken picture frames. I even made a tiny place where I could crawl inside the sculpture like a mangled womb, informing my parents that I wouldn't be returning to New York City because the unsightly mass had become my new home. Since they were the only ones who knew their child wasn't kidding, they chuckled and cautiously changed the subject.

The guests filed past with expressions of fear and wonder. Some dismissed my burgeoning sculpture as the antics of a seven-year-old, but some took it seriously, snapping shots of it with the artist standing proudly in front, wearing a gap-toothed smile. I certainly hadn't succeeded in rebuilding the island, but I did find my bliss. If other kids wanted toys, I wanted broken doll faces, dirty plastic bags that seemed oddly spiritual, ancient books with the words washed away, and shards of common kitchen appliances that looked like broken fingers. If other kids wanted princesses, I wanted monsters.

37

You know who else is totally obsessed with monsters? Lady Gaga spends her free time binge-watching monster movies and certainly sounds like an art monster when reflecting on her creative process: "When I am in an imaginative or creative mode, it sort of grabs me like a sleigh with a thousand horses and pulls me away and I just don't stop working." She also makes the connection between creativity and monstrosity herself, referring to herself as "Mother Monster" and calling her fans, "Little Monsters." She longs to be "an escape" for her acolytes, wants you, as a fan, to use her as, "the excuse to explore your identity. To be exactly who you are and to feel unafraid." When she screams, "paws up" at a concert, her followers know just what to do. They throw their hands skyward, crooking their fingers into monster claws, reaching for everything possible.

Gaga also dramatizes the connection the writers I've mentioned have made between the creative act of a mother popping out children and a mom popping out pages/artworks. Gaga confided to a *Vanity Fair* interviewer that she fears having lovers steal her creativity through her vagina. This image of innovation and creation itself as a distinctly female-identified form, and as having connections to a woman's reproductive organs/reproductive power is key to my examination of Lady Gaga but also to my exploration of women, creativity, and monsters overall. Gaga didn't arrive at the Grammys in an enormous egg for nothing: she wanted you to know she gave birth to that performance.

The link between Lady Gaga, her art, and bodily creation wasn't lost on Anna Maxymiw, who found creative impetus in Gaga's vagina statement, citing it as her reason to, as the title of her *Washington Post* article puts it, "Give Up Dating—and Finish My Book." In the essay, Maxymiw outlines the history of women's writing being plundered for men's use, and wives/ girlfriends typing up or editing husband's/ boyfriend's manuscripts instead of working on their own, including her own past with this, and her consequent decision, with that Gaga-vagina comment in mind, to stop dating and finish her darn book.

Maxymiw closes the essay with this: "I'll never forget Gaga's statement: It was weird and wonderful, blazing and brash, and it gave me freedom to release myself from the constraints of society's expectations regarding a woman's singleness. In that quote, I saw my own creative aspirations churning. I found the freedom I needed to become a writer." This sentiment echoes the response Gaga hopes to elicit from her fans, with one key addition so crucial to my work here: Gaga adds monsters to the mix.

The monster has long been tied to women who march outside the expected gender and sexuality borders, whether that be because they love other women or don't socially present the way "women" are "supposed to." When interviewed, Gaga's fans describe themselves as a merry band of "outcasts," "freaks," "misfits," who identify as, "different," "unique," and "weird."

The art monster is also a state of mind, a mode of positioning yourself vis-a-vis your own art. Jill Soloway writes, in the (sadly, now defunct; too witchy?) *Lenny Letter* about what she refers to as being a "weird girl," which I read as another form of, or at least a close cousin to, the art monster. It's important to note that Soloway identifies as non-binary, using they/them pronouns, and thus living outside the traditional gender cave. I therefore read this weird girl figure, like the witch and female monster in general, as one that transcends any conventional notion of gender. In addition to its connection to the word *queer,* the word *weird* has been linked to both witches and prophesy over time, as in Shakespeare's visionary Weird Sisters, who also lived beyond gender norms.

Soloway's piece was more battle cry of a brave soul in the wilderness than your typical web essay, exploring how we're all on trial for our weirdness. Soloway's response to this is the creation of art "with a sort of weaponizing feel, something zealous meant to raise hackles." Monstrous. There's nothing a woman can do that threatens the world more than marching outside the lines of definition. There's a reason they used to mark the unknown land in ancient maps with the very telling text, "Here There Be Monsters."

This weird girl concept is older than Shakespeare's wonderful Weird Sisters, before the first woman was ever accused of being a witch, even, but this particular *Lenny* essay refers to Soloway's television show (created with Sarah Gubbins), *I Love Dick,* and the source novel of the same name by Chris Kraus that I mentioned earlier. In particular, Soloway's piece refers to the fifth episode of the show, "A Short History of Weird Girls," which is a televisual masterpiece. It's a piece of fiction that feels almost documentary in its surveying of the experience of various women. This piece of television meditates on the intricacies and ferocity of female-identified life. Both the TV show and book *I Love Dick* explore women embracing their inner "monsters," which is yet another way of referring to their inner "weird girls." Each of the women in the "A Short History of Weird Girls" episode stares right into the camera and tells me the history of her desire—the story I always want to hear whenever I meet any woman, especially the weird ones.

Sometimes I meet a woman and there's this electric current between us like a third person in the room—a haunting of connection. In the rare cases I've felt this (probably a handful of times in my life), I've imagined she could feel it, too. Maybe it's a kind of shared language between women the world regards as, for lack of a better term, just "too much," for their husbands or girlfriends or boyfriends or wives or parents or work buddies. Just too much. Monstrous. So many of the women writers I mentally curated I saw later were ones I would guess would be drawn to the creative implications of the monstrous as opposed to repelled by them. Then I saw it: I was building a coven.

40

Lady Gaga articulates a clear connection between her monstrous message for her fans and the creative output where she hopes it leads: "This is the Manifesto of Little Monster. There is something heroic about the way my fans operate their cameras. So precisely, so intricately and so proudly. Like Kings writing the history of their people, is their prolific nature that both creates and procures what will later be perceived as the kingdom." Like so many of the women I've been obsessively studying, and like I have for years, Gaga looks not only to the monster in general but also to Mary Shelley's monster extraordinaire, *Frankenstein*, in particular—and to Shelley herself.

One of the many things that's so fascinating about Gaga's unreleased song, alternately called "Frankensteined" and "Frankenstein," is that the only way it's seen the light, so to speak, is in a few stolen moments where Gaga sang lines from it for fans backstage during her Joanne World Tour. It almost seems as though the song of the female monster has the same survival odds at the female monster herself. What happens to the female monster in the book, *Frankenstein*? Dr. Frankenstein finds the idea of her reproducing and making more lady monsters so terrible that he destroys her. In the movie, *Bride of Frankenstein,* she only survives for a bit, and here it's the male monster who does away with her because she doesn't want him back.

As in the case of Gaga's vaginal creativity quip, Shelley, too, connects literary production with biological production in intriguing ways. Mary Shelley functions like a case study of the art monster. Shelley read horror stories about ghosts and monsters, and then wrote *Frankenstein* after Byron challenged the group of writers they were hanging out with to write a ghost story. Shelley had lost her mother to childbirth, lost her own baby soon before and was caring for a five-month-old at the time of writing the book. She ended up writing a book about a monster that can simultaneously be read as a book about three kinds of creation: the creation of an actual monster, the creation of a book, and the creation of a child.

At the same time, Shelley's own creation monsters her, as she's faced constantly with the question of what kind of monster she had to be to write a book like that while she was supposed to be taking care of that baby, to write a book about a monster, or to write a book at all. She faces these accusations in the 1831 introduction, sticking up for the book, her "hideous progeny," and essentially penning an early female art monster manifesto in the process. So Shelley was simultaneously the art monster who wrote the book but also a writer capturing in text the metaphysics and creative process of the art monster. When I re-read *Frankenstein* years later, its ties to questions of creativity and motherhood seemed more pressing now that I was a mother myself.

My kids and I share a fascination with the monster. Or perhaps it's more precise to say that, like most children, mine are both drawn to and repelled by monsters. I chase them around the house while roaring loudly and they love it. We tell monster stories together for hours. It's funny because I can see even now how we're building the basis for their lifelong relationship to monsters and to narrative.

My children always want stories with some sort of monster in them, even if they must pay the price of being scared at bedtime. I tell them that this is just how adults feel about the monstrous. I don't tell them that this is the childhood equivalent of Julia Kristeva's notion of abjection. Monsters are the part of our world and ourselves that we alternately caress and push away, that play of disgust and desire that lives, as Kristeva says of abjection, "beyond the limits of the thinkable," which is exactly where I want to go with my writing. Yeah, I don't tell them that.

41

My own metamorphosis came about as I followed my guides—my art monster coven of women. Sure, I had always loved monsters and writing, but it wasn't until I had to fight for my art against a torrent of motherhood's many duties, pressures, and expectations that threatened to annihilate my writing that I truly transformed from pleasing young woman into art monster. Okay, so I'm a work in progress and much braver on the page. I still have to edit out the apologies in all that I do and am, but hopefully I'm on my way.

The monster is about transgressing borders, bodies, and identities, which is also what writing does for me. So I tell my children these stories that create a world for them in which they can never truly live, but almost, almost, and this is what makes it shimmer so. I create for them an inner womb of stories, since mine is no longer in season, which they can carry with them always, populated by myths and monsters, just as my parents did for me.

During the day, my children beg me to play the monster and pursue them, bumbling, wrapped in beach towels, around the living room. But at night they become afraid of the monster. Before bed, we do the various ornate rituals that enable them to actually go the fuck to sleep and not fear things that go bump in the night. This involves me squishing into their tiny beds and holding onto them like all our lives depend on it. I've never been able to do anything at half-mast, particularly not when it comes to adoring these screwy, marvelous little people who were somehow gifted to me. And then it starts: the monster questions: "Are there monsters on the moon?" "Are there any nice monsters?" One night I really just want to go to sleep, so I tell them, "You don't have to be afraid of monsters because I'm queen of the monsters, Mommy Monster, and they're all afraid of me." As I'm leaving the room, I hear a little voice, my daughter's, "Love you, Mommy Monster." And it just sounds so right.

42

In addition to her "Little Monster" fans, Lady Gaga does want to have biological children as well in the future (I foresee some sibling rivalry on the part of her fan base)—lots of them, in fact, three at least. She imagines it will be, "like having three little monsters with me all the time." But not yet. Fittingly, she once dismissed pregnancy rumors with this tweet, "Yeah, I'm pregnant with #LG6"—at the time, her next album.

In the case of Mary Shelley, the monster is a central character in her work who actually gets to speak (rare for a monster in a text), but this monster also functions as a metaphor for the creative process of writing itself and even the complex and wounding process by which that writing is received. Even the fact that the same actress plays both Mary Shelley and the female monster in *Bride of Frankenstein* reveals this supposed bond between female writer and monster—and certainly the female writer who writes of the monster. Gaga channels this whole sensibility in the "Frankenstein/Frankensteined" song.

In the "Frankenstein/Frankensteined" track, remarkably, Gaga's not playing the role of Frankenstein's male creature, but rather the female monster, referred to as his "Bride" in both book and movie. Notably, though, Gaga makes clear that she's nobody's wife. As the lyrics go: "Now I'm living the crime, crime, crime/ Call me Mother Monster I am not a bride." Maybe a woman being nobody's bride *is* the crime.

43

Unlike in the book *Frankenstein* and the movie *Bride of Frankenstein*, Gaga's version explores her identity as the female monster who never got to survive in the other narratives, but who lives on here. This song, then, creates an alternate reality, a safe space, in which the woman monster lives to tell her story, lives to dance to the beat of her own "twisted" rhythms and create, create, create.

In this revision, the female monster has either reanimated herself or never let herself be torn apart by a man in the first place. Perhaps she did the tearing apart instead, and here she is, not only alive, but singing, goddammit. What's more, in the book, the reason Dr. Frankenstein felt a duty to destroy the she-monster was because she could procreate and unleash on the earth a race of other monsters, maybe even—gasp—lady ones. So, in this female empowerment fantasy, Gaga has survived and become Mother Monster to what we can only imagine will become a gaggle of "little monsters," at once her art and what she calls her fans, as though she's the creator of her own monstrous fanbase. When Gaga swears off being the "bride," it reminds me of the only name we're ever given for the female protagonist of Offill's *Dept of Speculation,* "The Wife." The Wife mourns her art lost in a fog of domesticity, but not Gaga.

Gaga's not about being the wifey who doesn't get to be creative. She may mother, but it's her own self, her own music, and even her own fans to which she gives birth. It's all in the service of art, not domesticity, not the perfectly kept home. Her insistence that she's not a bride seems key here in terms of the art monster. The monster is the woman who pursues her needs and wants that don't fit with the aims of society—like a woman who doesn't want to have kids, or a woman who does but still wants to be badass (that's me).

44

Kim Brooks reasons that making art and mothering may be incompatible because "the point of art is to unsettle, to question, to disturb what is comfortable and safe. And that shouldn't be anyone's goal as a parent." On this issue, I fall more in the Rufi Thorpe camp, who writes, "If Kim Brooks worries that the job of art is to unsettle and the job of a mother is to soothe, perhaps there is no more unsettling solution than to insist she can do both, that there is, in fact, no conflict there, that motherhood itself is dark and uncharted and frightening. What if, in fact, motherhood is a boon to the artist? What if writing motherhood is the frontier, is the uncharted territory into which we must step if literature is to advance?"

In her song, "Bloody Mary," Gaga belts out, "We are not just Art for Michelangelo to carve, he can't rewrite the agro of my furied heart." She puts this in more direct terms when she says, "Some women choose to follow men, and some women choose to follow their dreams. If you're wondering which way to go, remember that your career will never wake up and tell you that it doesn't love you anymore." This seems to be what Maxymiw took away from Gaga as well when she stopped dating to finish her book.

In "Frankenstein/Frankensteined," Gaga sings of waking up chained in a little room, presumably imprisoned by Dr. Frankenstein, but her bright aura shines through the darkness, allowing her to smash the windows and escape this enclosure. I think of glass ceilings but also the pretty little glass boxes in which women are placed, sometimes living whole lives in there. It's not merely older women/mothers who feel this either. When I taught a monster-themed writing college course recently, many of the young women wrote about the monster as a potential means of escaping, of breaking out of the container of "womanhood."

45

One day I woke to find that I was no longer comfortable in my own lady container—that I never was—and that my whole life was becoming secretly untenable on some level. And so I turned toward the monstrous, in my writing at least.

William Strunk Jr., who wrote the book we all read in composition classes, *The Elements of Style*, believed the reader was a drowning man in a swamp. He thought it was the job of the good writer to save him through the clarity of his written movements. (I guess the drowning woman can just be left in the swamp.) While this sounds good and all, it doesn't describe my favorite books whatsoever.

On the contrary, I want the writer to throw me right into the swamp, show me everything. The most creative works force me to remake my notion of what the world is, what art is, what I am. The result is writing that gestures towards another world outside or within me for which there may not even be official language. Show me something I've never seen before. But, please, don't just show me your dick because that' s not what I'm talking about, and I, too, have Internet. Not that I'll look away. I never do.

46

But it's not the hackneyed "money shot" that I'm after, nor is it the one-dimensional Instagram selfie. I'm more interested in a confession that amounts to an opening of the head by way of knife and placing the brain matter on the page (and this is where the horror comes in): confess to me how it all connects and how it got that way inside you, take things apart and put them back together, make me pant for more. I suppose I should be careful about what I'm asking you to show me brain-wise, though. While reading *Winnie the Pooh* with my daughter recently, my mom asked her if she knew what a brain was, after they read that word together: "Yes, a brain is what mama got to pee with."

Today I saw a heart as I was going down the subway steps. It was a sticker, red as a real heart but not beating. I reached out and touched it as I was walking down. I didn't even stop to see who might be looking. I think this may be because I'm older now and so I've decided I can do what I want, at least as far as fake hearts are concerned. This gesture was meant to say that I'm beating, out for blood but not in a violent sense. But what kind of violence was I after? The kind that hurt nobody but could make readers tremble as if before grace. Warning: this book will break all the rules. It must.

Every morning I tell myself, "This time you'll write a legible story where things happen and then people will buy it," but I always end up creating another weird piece of writing. In December 2017 a violent storm called Caroline swept the UK. I had to keep telling myself, "It's not you. You're blameless and right here. You crave intellectual upheaval, not real harm." I write because there are certain things that would explode me if I didn't express them. These detonators are everywhere–from the unreal appearance of the water that falls from my shower every morning to the ugly beauty of ballerina feet. I must do something with this sensation, or I'll burst, so I write about it. I don't merely go to watch them in the theaters; I am my own horror movie.

47

Ultimately, I felt I either had to embrace the art monster and find creative possibility in this monstrous territory or not take up that writerly time and space at all. I found my way by collecting women who telegraphed a sort of monstrous creativity to get me through my days and push me to create when I wanted to go sob into a pile of dirty onesies. Melissa A. Click , Hyunji Lee, and Holly Willson Holladay write that, "Through their involvement with the community built around Lady Gaga, Little Monsters have reappropriated the term 'monster' by re-articulating its outsider status to inner strength and originality."

Gaga's not alone in her art monster project by a long shot. She's part of a reclamation project I'm seeing unfold before my very eyes: the reclaiming of the monster by women, the reversing of its negative valence, and the harnessing of this monster towards the ends of ferocious creativity. See: all the feminist books on monsters and witches lately.

This is my chronicle of my journey to art monsterhood— my move away from being pleasing and towards being unruly, my move away from being looked at to looking, my move away from being written to being a writer. With this book I just hope that some woman sitting at home, feeling small and terrified, even though nobody knows that secret about her, will feel a little less alone reading this. I want to find this woman, reach out and mother her. I would rub her back and say, "It's just me and you now, kiddo."

48

But I haven't been telling you the whole story. There's another reason I became acquainted with the monster at such a young age: trauma. Sorrow itself, or melancholy, was once thought of as a case of dark spirits circulating in the body—proof that our bodies and minds were the original haunted houses.

I'm not going to go into it in specifics because it's mine, and also it's not how I write. For me, at least, trauma and being an artist requires that you derange reality, that you fragment it, make of it a mosaic, a collage, a monster.

Something problematic in the art monster mythos is women's identification with the monster when they have also suffered at the hands of monstrous men, as Claire Dederer's essay captures. Some called it troubling the way Dederer's essay blends together monstrous men and the female art monster, and it is, but it's also a crucial question of this ideological terrain. Female art monsters often need to take back what male art monsters or just male monsters have stolen from them. I'm not saying that every woman has been traumatized, but most have had something taken from them, something that they need to get back at any cost.

I can tell you about taking back what was stolen but I won't tell you everything that happened. What I need to speak of is a question of aftermath, and how it all got mixed up with the monstrous in my mind, how I needed to engage with horror as a therapy and as a way out, but also how I decided that my mode of survival would be to make something out of what had happened. I had to find a way to make my suffering creative, to ensure that I could *do something* with it. I saw the monster as manifold pieces of what had happened to me all contained in one uncategorizable body. I also saw the monster as my own strength and creativity—my ticket to my favorite form of alchemy: turning shit into gold.

Then more and more gets made, and I can feel that instead of withering to a crisp, I have learned to turn to what I think of as my personal and beloved monster: this magic whereby I turn pain into invention. Welcome to my house of horrors. You can see my youthful ache on display. This is why I shivered as I read Plath's "Lady Lazarus." But I reject the story that I'm now a "sad girl" writer because I enjoy Plath's writing. I refuse it. This is not the story of how I gave in; it's the story of how I grew into a composite creature, a monster in the best possible way.

I have lived my life trying to hide my trauma, deciding it would make me dirty and disgusting in the eyes of society and so exposed. Although I'm sure anybody who's ever read my writing can guess that there's something pretty ugly there, I like to avoid discussing what my trauma is because, like most traumatized people, I am secretive, but obviously not that secretive since I am a writer. This oxymoronic combo has led to my writing style—what I like to call memoir as glimpsed in a fun house mirror. I leave little traces of who I am for you to parse apart. This is how I keep myself safe from predators. Or, as Mary Ann

Doane puts it, "The femme fatale is the figure for a certain discursive unease, a potential epistemological trauma. For her most striking characteristic, perhaps, is the fact that she never really is what she seems to be. She harbors a threat which is not entirely legible, predictable, or manageable. In thus transforming the threat of the woman into a secret, something which must be aggressively revealed, unmasked, discovered, the figure is fully compatible with the epistemological drive of narrative, the hermeneutic structuration of the classical text." So when I say, "read me like a book," I mean it. Also, it's okay if you don't "get" that quotation. I had to read it about ten times before it started speaking to me.

I am the type of person who has a love-hate relationship with leaving my house in the morning, with being outside the safety of my study, which is also my kids' room. How I put stuff up on social media only to feel ashamed of too much self-exposure, too much *look at me*, Too much, *I am so pleased to announce* publication announcements and how I can't help but picture the people who are having a high rejection week reading it and wanting to knife the screen because I've been there. So I want to cancel myself often, am so ashamed of the way I show myself in each new book that it makes me want to throw up, so shy to teach or do a reading that it turns my pale vampire skin fuchsia. At the same time, I want to show myself to the world so badly it's a compulsion, at least through my words. What is that? I recently made a meme about being an introverted person who teaches and writes for a living. It's a gif of some underground animal poking its head out and then scampering back inside its hole. You can just look at that to understand me and save a lot of time reading this book.

49

A large part of how I've come to survive is through being a writer, and writing in the (often lyrical, fragmented, fractured, whatever you want to call it) essay form in particular. In his foundational 1910 work "On the Nature and Form of the Essay," Georg Lukács imagines the act of essay making as "an event of the soul," "a conceptual reordering of life," and essays as "intellectual poems." I also teach the essay and am currently obsessed with the hermit crab and braided forms of the essay.

Susan Griffin's braided essay "Red Shoes" always stuns me. Even though I have made a career out of the hubris of claiming to be able to explain things, I cringe at the thought of trapping Griffin's creative intellectual event in any sort of descriptive language—especially since the essay meditates on just this sort of enclosure. Suffice it to say it's a doozy of an essay. I suppose I should give you some sense of what it's about. Let's just say it interweaves Griffin's childhood memories with wolfishly smart insight into both the significance of women's lives and the life of signification itself.

To give you just a wee taste, she begins the essay like so: "The imprisonment which was at one and the same time understood as the imprisonment of the female mind has a larger boundary, and that is the shape of thought itself within Western civilization. It is an early memory. Red shoes. Leather straps crisscrossing. The kind any child covets. That color I wanted with the hot desire of a child."

"Red Shoes" explores the memory of these red shoes, of childhood becoming and trauma, and plays all of this against its own ingenious structure. We can see already from the above quote how Griffin reflects the "imprisonment of the female mind" in those "leather straps crisscrossing." She ultimately transforms her words on the page into something larger that I believe every good essay should be: a slice of living thought that reflects on its own thinking and being—and then zooms out to examine the structure of thinking and being itself.

50

Another huge part of my survival has been my edgy (ribald? inappropriate?) sense of humor. The past two years have been anything but funny. And yet, to remake my mind during the pandemic, as Covid strains and sociopolitical atrocities floated through my news feed, I turned to female stand-up comedians.

It all started with Tig Notaro's 2012 comedy album *Live*. Recorded four days after Notaro's breast cancer diagnosis, the album has been described as "anti-comedy"—in addition to the cancer diagnosis, Notaro shares she's just lost her mother, and that the hospital accidentally sent her dead mom a satisfaction survey. Then she uses the survey's form to structure the segment.

At the time, I was preparing to teach a creative nonfiction class on the hermit crab form. As I toggled between the album and Brenda Miller and Suzanne Paola's definition of the hermit crab essay as one that "appropriates other forms as an outer covering," I started seeing Notaro's set as a hermit crab essay—a comedy set in the form of a hospital satisfaction survey, in the form of tragedy, in the form of creative nonfiction. Both the hermit crab and stand-up comedy forms hinge on their ability to surprise. They recast something you thought you knew in a whole new framework that highlights both its familiarity and its strangeness.

Stand-up comedy isn't usually included under the creative nonfiction umbrella, perhaps because of its performative element, or maybe because comedy still gets labeled as a "low art" (because snobbery) and creative nonfiction as a "high one." But it definitely should be.

The current work of women stand-up comics reflects and builds on what women creative nonfiction writers are doing in terms of telling important stories—ranging from childbirth to trauma—in ways that expand what's possible in storytelling. Stand-up comedians and creative nonfiction writers may work in different arenas, but the impulse at the center of their work—to present their own experiences in inventive and transformative ways—is in many ways the same. And now, at a time of so much suffering, these writers' ability to communicate trauma in particular is more crucial than ever, revolutionary even.

In a *New York Times* interview, Hannah Gadsby—another comic whose work has been labelled "anti-comedy"— says of stand-up, "There does have to be a revolution of form in order to accommodate different voices," and a revolution there has been.

51

Historically, male comics have built a joke arsenal on the myth of the mirthless woman. In particular, women's bodies and what they emit (see: childbirth) have often been cited as part of why ladies are incapable of killing at comedy. Jerry Lewis said, in 2000: "A woman doing comedy doesn't offend me but sets me back a bit ... I think of her as a producing machine that brings babies into the world." In his 2007 *Vanity Fair* polemic "Why Women Aren't Funny," Christopher Hitchens included this gem: "For women, reproduction is, if not the only thing, certainly the main thing. Apart from giving them a very different attitude to filth and embarrassment, it also imbues them with the kind of seriousness and solemnity at which men can only goggle."

To claim reproducing makes women squeamish about "filth and embarrassment" reflects a crucial misunderstanding of the birthing and mothering process—experiences the current crop of women comedians explore in vivid terms. As anyone with a Netflix subscription could tell you, one of the most remarkable aspects of women's current stand-up is how much of its volcanic hilarity comes from foregrounding the very thing that supposedly makes a woman unfunny, her body. Ali Wong, for instance, who wowed audiences by appearing onstage hugely pregnant not once but twice, nails the havoc childbirth wreaks on the body in her 2018 special *Hard Knock Wife*. The container of comedy doesn't force Wong to rise above the bodily, to move on, to grow up; rather, she dwells in that abject realm of motherly blood, guts, pee, poop, and milk until it becomes its own form of transcendence.

A Wong set is a front row ticket to motherhood. For example, a clogged milk duct leads to a visit from the dreaded lactation consultant (who nobody has nailed better in the history of language), that "white NPR-listener with dreadlocks named Indigo, that you have to pay $200 to rush over to your house and Roto-Rooter your titty." Similarly, Amy Schumer, in her 2019 special *Growing*, draws us in so close that we get why she loves us but hopes our cars crash if we had good pregnancies after she spent hers *Exorcist*-style puking from hyperemesis gravidarum. And in her 2017 special *Mother Inferior*, Christina Pazsitsky telegraphs how hard parenting can be to the extent that when she admits she loves her kid but also wants to go into the bathroom and push a Q-Tip right into her brain, we don't judge her; we raise our Q-Tips in solidarity.

Sure, stand-up comedy has an embodied element that writing on the page doesn't. But even if we "page writers" don't have access to that performative aspect, the biggest craft lesson I've learned from stand-up is the importance of immersive, demonstrative verbal depictions of experience that transport the reader/viewer into the world you're building with your words. A.K.A. good old *showing not telling*. For instance, rather than being told breastfeeding is tough, we're immersed in the florid verbal imagery of Wong's clogged milk duct description until it comes to feel like our own. I could do a whole lecture on the importance of showing versus telling in writing craft or we could do a little experiment where I show versus tell. What's more convincing—saying that breastfeeding a baby is challenging, or describing it (like Wong does) as a "savage ritual that just reminds you that your body is a cafeteria now"? That's what I thought.

52

One of the most striking techniques in writing of any kind right now is how women are using humor to address the body and sexual trauma in ingenious ways that rewrite the old victim narrative. Witness Patricia Lockwood's poem "Rape Joke," which nails rape culture even in its first few lines:

The rape joke is that you were 19 years old.
The rape joke is that he was your boyfriend.
The rape joke it wore a goatee. A goatee.
Imagine the rape joke looking in the mirror, perfectly reflecting back itself, and grooming itself to look more like a rape joke. "Ahhhh," it thinks. "Yes. A goatee."
No offense.

Even now, unfortunately, when a woman speaks seriously about her experience of sexual assault, she's often dismissed as a spoilsport or sourpuss. So, instead, Lockwood plops the reader down at the center of both the rape experience and how that rape experience will be culturally received—inviting you to visualize, even to personify, the joke that it will become, told by some dude. Except that Lockwood has gotten ahead of it, crafting the rape joke herself, from her own experience and in the form of a poem, no less. Lockwood's lines also demonstrate that writing doesn't have to be technically categorized as either comedy or creative nonfiction to do some of that same work.

In her 2018 special, *Rape Jokes,* Cameron Esposito says we're not yet discussing these issues of sexual trauma; we're at the precipice, and she wants to push us over the edge. On this topic, in *Hysterical,* the 2021 documentary on women comedians, stand-up veteran Margaret Cho says the challenge is to use suffering like paint, the dark to contrast the light, which pairs nicely with stand-up comic Iliza Shlesinger's point, in the same documentary, that the best comic delivery comes when, in a manner "almost melodic," you change it up, mix registers, go from shallow to deep, low to high, and back again.

In *Hysterical,* Cho also recounts how a man locked her in her dressing room and tried to rape her. She focuses on the jokey aspect of a guy half her size trying to accost her, but she also reveals she's been raped in the past and molested as a child, so we can see the very real emotions hovering beyond the joke, maybe even more starkly for having arrived via the side street of humor. This layover gives us time to reflect, creates an augmented mental space for us to work though Cho's material, which melds with our own, creating one ugly conceptual baby Ali Wong would really have a field day with.

53

In her 2017 special *A Speck of Dust*, Sarah Silverman recounts a disturbing tale about her drunk sister: puking in a coed dorm, she thinks she feels someone pulling down her underwear. Our hearts sink; we think we know where this story is headed. Silverman constructs the joke so that the audience is in her sister's place—feeling the dread most women have felt, the fear that their body could be violated. And then, she breaks the tension. It eventually dawns on Silverman's very drunk sister that it's her *own* hands pulling her underwear down. What a relief. (As she soils herself.)

I initially hated this bit because it seemed to make light of rape, but I came to see that there were two possible ways of interpreting it. Possibility number one: Silverman thinks rape is funny(!), which would not be so surprising given that rape jokes have long been a mainstay of the comedy circuit. In fact, in 2012 Silverman joked that rape was "like the safest area to talk about in comedy. Cause who's going to complain about a rape joke? Rape victims? They don't even report rape," on different stages but on the same night that comedian (?) Daniel Tosh had this to say to a female audience member who told him rape was never funny: "Wouldn't it be funny if that girl got raped by like 5 guys right now?"

But here's possibility number two, which is a more likely explanation: Silverman doesn't think rape is funny. Rather, she hopes her material will serve as an empathy exercise for men (the ones who haven't been raped, at any rate) and a relief for women of "the tension they feel because of the fear of rape," as sociologist Carol Mitchell characterizes the rape joke. Like Lockwood and pretty much every woman ever, Silverman might also know that when women write serious treatises on this subject, men write them off as sad sacks and killjoys, and she may think this joke, this way of telling it slant, is a more useful way in.

After Silverman tells this unsettling story, she points out how scared the audience was before she comforted them by letting them know her sister hadn't been raped. Silverman has thus controlled the comic tension intricately, structuring the joke to emphasize, you guessed it, *showing over telling*. And thus she has also effectively given a demonstration of a key Kantian philosophical premise of humor (what?!): "Laughter is an affection arising from the sudden transformation of a strained expectation into nothing."

54

Perhaps no other comedian has done more to subvert both rape culture and the conventional, often misogynistic, form of comedy itself than Hannah Gadsby. Gadsby is the stand-up comedian who, in her 2018 comedy-breaking special *Nanette*, famously dared to simultaneously be unfunny (while also being hilarious) and quit the industry.

Gadsby opens *Nannette* by sharing that she doesn't feel safe in a small town. This alone reverses the common lore and is just the first in a series of profound reversals. Because, of course, for people who inhabit the margins, as Gadsby formulates it, a small town just might be the most dangerous place on earth. She jokes that small-town folks view her as a "trickster" after initially taking her for a man. Later, it becomes clear that this trickster sensibility secretly structures the whole set; Gadsby tells the story of a guy who almost beat her up for hitting on his girlfriend, but then relented when he realized Gadsby was a woman. But here's the twist: that's not what actually happened.

Throughout the show, Gadsby builds to the game-changing conclusion that comedy's recipe—setup and punchline—invariably leaves out the ending, the real story. And so, Gadsby remakes the comic equation. She circles back to that tale about the guy and cuts out any conventional notion of a punchline (aha, you're a lady, so I won't hit you!), revealing instead that he did in fact beat the crap out of her and nobody did a damn thing about it. She shares this, along with sexual assaults she's undergone, using the complete narrative structure (beginning, middle, and end) that comedy often eschews in favor of a punchline. She thereby creates a narrative monster that is more expressively powerful and, yes, even funnier, for being hybrid—the head of a joke with the body of storytelling. As she admits in her next special, *Douglas*, "I know better than anyone that what I did with *Nanette* was not technically comedy. But I'm also not a fucking idiot. I wanted that show to have an audience, and a broad audience, and if that meant I had to trick people ... by calling it comedy ... that's technically a joke."

Notably, what she does in both shows, though differently, is also an audacious form of creative nonfiction.

In *Douglas*, which centers on an adult autism diagnosis, Gadsby reverses the maneuver she pulled in *Nannette*. Instead of leaving out a crucial conclusive element, she previews the show's whole configuration, the very structure of the show an ode to neurodiversity. In *Nannette*, she conceals; in *Douglas*, she reveals. But both shows somehow end up in that same space of concealment and revelation, of something being recast—comedy, thought, narrative, the body, what could be. In this way, Gadsby's stand-up is like a magic show: she shows us the card at the beginning of the show, and yet it's a surprise when it emerges again at the end, identical and yet transformed by the power of narrative. "I don't tell you this," she says after sharing her trauma, "so you think of me as a victim. I am not a victim. I tell you this because my story has value." She tells us, "There is nothing stronger than a broken woman who has rebuilt herself."

55

Another comedian who knows a little something about conceptually rebuilding the body in innovative ways is the intrepid Wanda Sykes. In her 2006 comedy album, *Sick and Tired*, she poses the following thought experiment (which riffs on an earlier bit by stand-up trailblazer Elayne Boosler): "Wouldn't it be wonderful if our pussies were detachable? ... Just think of the freedom that you'll have." She then mimes the wild liberty of jogging at night without worrying about getting jumped by a man. Next, she imagines being approached and announcing giddily, "Uh, I left it at home. Sorry, I have absolutely nothing of value on me. I'm pussy-less!" To me, this is innovation, a joke that builds a new world. I also find it strangely redemptive to watch, as though for those moments I am also freed of the baggage of this particular problematic body part.

When it comes to revising notions about woman as victim and turning the sexual assault tables, one of the most arresting moments in recent stand-up comes from Marina Franklin. In her 2019 special *Single Black Female*, Franklin describes seeing some guy jerking off to her on the subway. Through sheer comic technique, Franklin gives this unfortunately familiar scenario a *Fight Club*-worthy twist ending. When faced with this man using his penis as a weapon, she doesn't flee. Oh no. She stares that phallus down, sexually sizing it up, licking her lips, playing predator right back, instead of victim. The masturbator finds himself in slippery ontological territory because

Franklin has now broken the rules of public masturbation, bypassed the box of definition. *What even is she?*

Franklin, who is also the host of the podcast "Friends Like Us," calls herself "bilingual" for being able to speak like an African American woman and a White woman, and here she demonstrates a different kind of bilingualism. She speaks predator to the predator and what happens? "Now it's *my* story," she says—because it happened to her, but also in the sense that women have been taking back control of the narrative in the post-#MeToo era.

"Oh, I made *him* uncomfortable," Franklin declares, doing an impression of the guy turning around to try to finish himself off. In the scene she conjures, he keeps looking back at her, scared, saying, "Ma'am, this is not how this works." If you've ever had a man do this (or worse) to you, or even if you just like funny stuff, you need to see this special now. As a human woman who's experienced her fair share of such men, I can't tell you what this scene meant to me; it was so much more therapeutic than all the therapy or even the serious essays I've read on the topic. Throughout the show, Franklin has been searching for her "Black Girl Magic," and this carnivalesque ability to remake language, the power structure, maybe even eventually the world itself—just might be it.

For Franklin to turn the tables on the masturbator is funny, to be sure, but for me it also deconstructs and reconstructs assumptions about how everything else— our thoughts, our world, our writing, our understanding of culture—might be rearranged, remade, seen anew. Not only does humor not make something less brilliant or creative but, in many cases, I'd argue it makes it more so. Comedy works by fusing unexpected qualities together, through irony, subversion, lacunae, silence, and speech. I view innovation and genius as the making of unusual, never-before-seen connections, and this is exactly what the best comics—and creative nonfiction writers—do.

Although supposedly working in massively different genres and arenas, both stand-up comics and creative nonfiction writers use their own experiences, presented in inventive ways, to break down and rebuild, Frankenstein-style, notions about both their bodies and the body of narrative. Both groups explore trauma by taking on the form of its fragmented structure, using their ordeal as the engine of their craft, presenting how the world has tried to tear them apart. But then—and this is key in a time of trauma that calls for a reinvention of storytelling that foregrounds resilience—through stunning reversals, they show how they put themselves back together into more ingenious forms.

56

And comedy's flipside, horror, has also been equally therapeutic for me. Oh God, how hard it was to watch those blasted Freddy Kruger movies, what with the whole molesting ghoul rising from the dead to come back and attack the kids through their dreams. But I also found watching these movies to be a counterintuitive and cheaper form of therapy—a way of working through things in a safe space in certain ways, a way of at least thinking that I can find creative seeds in traumatic horrific material that I call my insides, at least in my early life. Or was I just re-traumatizing myself when I watched those films?

I tried to tell myself that I had known the monstrous but that within the monstrous is the greatest genius, that somehow I would be a better writer for it, for having come back from the underworld to tell my story, come back with the scent of hell still on me, a whiff of forever and burnt toast. And maybe this is why Sylvia Plath's writing resonated with me. But, most of all, she always sounded like a fellow survivor to me.

Plath's "Poem for a Birthday" is rich with troubling experience to confront. It has elicited quite an array of interpretations. Julia Rose identifies the response it has received as falling "at the interface between denigration and sacrilisation of her writing... it seems that something troubling is being located in this sequence of poems by its reader on condition that it either destroys or sublates itself." Kristeva, for her part, would revel in the abject delights of the first section of Plath's poem: "In the marketplace they are piling dry sticks. / A thicket of shadows is a poor coat. I inhabit / The wax image of myself, a doll's body. / Sickness begins here: I am a dartboard for witches. / Only the devil can eat the devil out. / In the month of red leaves I climb to a bed of fire." Plath's speaker sets the stage in such a subtle way that we don't realize right away what's really happening: that the pyre being built is to burn a witch, and that the witch is the speaker, but also, I always felt, is me.

57

I usually can't watch horror movies that remind me too much of what I went through. In fact, although I enjoy cerebral haunted house movies and certain other kinds, probably about 60 percent of horror movies I can't watch. Like *Silence of the Lambs*. Watching it gave me weeks of nightmares that went something like this: a woman found at the bottom of a well, body turned bloody in luminous blades of light. I imagined that, extinguished, she tried to find her way, like Alice lost in Thunderland. Something about topography, a map fashioned from severed bits of skin. Man-made woman parts worn in private piracy of mind, raining down upon the earth, transforming many colors into rhyme. This the body, these the bones changing, the poet transfigured, when skin-grafted telephone poles call out softly in the wind. In the end, a snake-of-itself-eating put the world in the drum of her ear, and she was fallen. Or something like that.

60

Clearly, for me writing is all about monsters: monster as trauma to be exorcized, as plot, as inspiration, as creativity, as the thing I was both fleeing and running toward at the speed of light. It was also the brilliant work that could be made from all these broken pieces. I think I started a philosophy even as a little girl of befriending the monster, like evil and trauma and suffering was a continuum. I thought I could walk so far into my own pain that I would write my way back to life.

When I saw something that scared me as a child, I often raised a hand in a circle and looked at it through that "lens" and the spectacle would come into relief, at once clearer than ever and drastically distorted, rendered monstrous, horror creatures, and the fear would fall away. I see now that I had become its filmmaker. I had become the artist, the director, not the damsel in distress. Their monstrous moves suddenly controlled by me. This is how I made it through those moments that stay with me like my own skin. There are many fancy descriptions of PTSD, but essentially it means your monsters are always walking around with you. For me, then, there's this choice of whether to embrace them or not, whether to deploy them as members of my own army. The alternative is to be eaten.

61

In Offill's *Dept of Speculation,* "the wife" begins teaching her students creation myths. She tells them that when God is portrayed as the father he is said to be elsewhere, and when God is portrayed as the mother she's said to be everywhere. As Ovid knew only too well in his *Metamorphoses,* one definition of monstrosity has to do with transformation.

My favorite part about *Metamorphoses* is how it's not so much about multiple transformations, although of course that as well, but rather one long, rippling change. The alterations range across stories, with one part of a tale reaching in to change another, resulting in one long interrelated metamorphosis called life, that begins at the dawn of time and ends with the final metamorphosis: the spirit of the assassinated king Julius Caesar transforming into a star. Ovid was after origins.

And so was Freud, who referred to the riddle of the Sphinx as the question of where babies come from. But there was a second riddle the Sphinx is said to have posed: "There are two sisters: one gives birth to the other and she, in turn, gives birth to the first. Who are the two sisters?" The answer is "day and night."

This second riddle imagines a woman-only world where these sisters can give birth to each other rather than requiring the male "invasion" of metaphorical intercourse— placing narrative power firmly and eternally back in the hands of the ladies, and particularly the female monster.

Figures such as the Sphinx and the Medusa remind us that female monsters contain multitudes. They are about trauma, and the thrill and danger of desiring, seeing, knowing, and creating—whether it be the creation of potions, babies, or books.

62

Over at *LitHub*, Natalie Diaz curates a beautiful bi-monthly series of work by queer Indigenous women poets. One installment meditates on the art monster in a striking way. She introduces this installment with the hope that it will function like Mojave song-maps, which, "do not draw borders or boundaries, do not say *this* is knowable, or defined, or *mine*. Instead our maps use language to tell about our movements and wonderings (not wanderings) across a space, naming what has happened along the way while also compelling us toward what is waiting to be discovered, where we might go and who we might meet or become along the way." The first poem, from Noʻu Revilla, with the great title "Memory as Missionary Position," opens with a bang, demanding that we look upon this girl creature:

Inside the dress, there is a creature, she
                                    careful

is a cliff in a girl's body.
And the cliff was a lizard once still   turned
to rock she gazed too much like she

                        careful

had a kingdom inside.

Revilla's poem invites us to stare at this girl creature, into her dress even, while it warns us, with that repeated "careful," about the ramifications of this peering. Let's remember that looking in literature is rarely innocent and rarely goes unpunished.

This reverse-Medusa is herself turned to stone for the crime of too much gazing, for her gluttony of sight. But the questions pour forth after reading this work. Was this creature always stone, "a cliff in a girl's body"? Or did the stone come only after the staring? But before that she was a lizard. So maybe she was a stone lizard? This shifting lets us know we are not in fixed territory identity-wise.

In this sense, the opening to "Memory as Missionary Position" perfectly illustrates Diaz's introductory ambitions. It embodies that song-map quality of refusing to draw borders between this entity that is or has been a "creature" in a dress, a "cliff in a girl's body," a "lizard," and a "rock." As a poem, "Memory as Missionary Position" doesn't give us a traditional map that that tells us *what is*. Rather, it provides more of a speculative map, showing, in Diaz's terms, the motions of this woman-rock-creature through time, which raise questions about where she's been, *where she may be going*, and what other transformations she might undergo along the way. The sky's the limit.

If we unravel the central "character" of this poem, we find something astonishing that contains multitudes: a creature in a dress, a cliff who used to be a lizard, in a girl's body, in a dress, with a kingdom inside her. In the end, this creature, this poem, and the work of queer Indigenous women poets is similarly multifaceted, containing layer upon layer of identity that defies any strict definition, inviting us to go a-wondering.

68

Julia Kristeva describes her notion of abjection as that which, "disturbs identity, system, order: What does not respect borders, positions, rules. The in-between, the ambiguous, the composite." These books I love often defy definition, being described as everything from lyric essay and memoir to, as Sheila Heti does with *Heroines*, "composite creature." And what is a composite creature but a monster? There's a reason Phillip Lopate refers to the similarly hybrid form, the essay film, as a "centaur."

This makes sense to me since, mythologically speaking, Chiron was the centaur who educated gods and royalty. Machiavelli thought Chiron's pedagogical brilliance came from the very fact that he was a composite creature—part man, part beast, part gentle and intellectual and part brute force. I see it like this: to learn and create in profound ways, you need hybridity. The monster is part this, part that, part human and part something else we haven't even found thoughts for yet, which are precisely the terms in which we need to think of our greatest art creations.

What is it about some writing that makes me swear something inside me is expanding at a stunning rate, slowing down just long enough for me to pause inside myself and marvel at what's happening before whatever it is speeds off into the distance? What makes certain books so hauntingly good—good enough to make me want to, in the words of William H. Gass, "give up the blue things of this world in favor of the words which say them"?

In *Ulysses*, James Joyce writes, "The supreme question about a work of art is out of how deep a life does it spring. Paintings of Moreau are paintings of ideas. The deepest poetry of Shelley, the words of Hamlet bring our mind into contact with the eternal wisdom; Plato's world of ideas. All the rest is the speculation of schoolboys for schoolboys." So what separates the Shelleys from the schoolboys? There's no general definition of a great work because what we love and why we love it is a question for a therapist or biographer, but it's interesting to ponder the qualities that make most people gasp with pleasure when they read.

What am I searching for in these hours of the kind of reading that borders on madness? On rare occasions when I stay up late reading a brilliant book, I'm blessed with the slow realization of what it really is—its second self that waits for me to earn the knowledge of it. When I get the chills, I know it's coming. I feel my skin prickle and my hair rise, as if in salute to this book, whose grandeur appeared over time as I read, and then became a colossus overnight. Virginia Woolf writes in *The Waves,* "I was always going to the bookcase for another sip of the divine specific," and many a night I have reached for just that sort of celestial particular.

But, and this is crucial, the book, just like a person, can't try too hard, can't shout, "look at me, I'm gorgeous!" too loud or we start to wonder how lovely it truly is. As Maggie Nelson writes in *Bluets* (one of the works that effectively blew my mind), her book "will not say, Isn't X beautiful? Such demands are murderous to beauty . . . The most I want to do is show you the end of my index finger. Its muteness." What Nelson does (and I would argue all the greats do) is just this. It's the old "show, don't tell" writing advice taken to its wildest extent, a place in which the words all but fall away and leave you almost with the astounding experience itself.

At times I think a book's brilliance has to do with the pull of opposites. This could mean something as complex as the Hegelian notion of the idea (thesis) coming into contact with its opposition that at least partially undoes it (antithesis), and the haunting composite, the new order that rushes in as a result (synthesis). Maybe it's all about structure—those books which build their own structures inside you. Or it could be writing with, for example, a supreme, disciplined structure mixed suddenly with a mode that's entirely different–renegade, illegal even (in a writing sense, at least), anarchistic, inventive beyond the pale, a horse that's jumped the fence and has no intention of ever coming back.

Or it could be as simple as the pleasing cognitive dissonance of, for instance, a supremely ugly thing written about in the most supremely beautiful language (or the other way around).

Even if I can't precisely define what constitutes great writing, I can tell you without a shadow of a doubt, via Woolf again, writing in *The Waves*, how it makes me feel: "There was a star riding through clouds one night, and I said to the star, 'Consume me.'" I'm not saying I'm capable of writing like this, but it doesn't stop me from obsessively trying to get there. With this goal in mind, I like to gaze at something until my eyes go blurry and I start to see something else entirely—some obscure, bedimmed space I can only imagine is my own creativity. Then, at that intersection between my mind and that other one, I start writing.

69

I think of the kind of writing that results from this sort of exercise as a monster—fragmented, slasher-style, barely legal. I'd say it's a more modern sensibility that we can see in artworks such as *Body Scan* in which Erica Scourti photographed her body's parts with an iPhone and then ran them through Internet search engines— I think we can all agree this isn't something that would have happened in our grandparents' day—except look at the fragmenting presence of the monstrous in medieval lit.

Anne Sexton writes, "I was born / doing reference work in sin, and born / confessing it. This is what poems are: / with mercy for the greedy, / they are the tongue's wrangle, / the world's pottage, the rat's star." When I find work like this, I revere it because I know that to invent it some writer had to suture together a woman's head and a fish's haunches, so to speak.

When my father read me the Hans Christian Andersen fairy tale *The Little Mermaid* and later when I saw the movie, I wasn't spooked by the magnificent sea witch; I was riveted. What horrified me was the mermaid mutilating herself, giving up her tail and voice (her art) to get the prince. When Pat Carroll, who voiced Ursula the sea witch in the 1989 Disney film *The Little Mermaid*, first saw her own performance she felt frightened, recognizing in it shades of Margaret Hamilton as the Wicked Witch of the West.

I will never forget sitting in the front row of that movie

theater watching *The Little Mermaid*, wide-eyed, wondering what happened to her voice, to her discarded mermaid tail. Did the witch store it in the same seashell necklace where she kept the mermaid's voice? Since there was so little space in there, did they merge? On cold, lonely nights, would that lonely little fish tail sing to itself?

I could either be the beautiful mermaid who gets her voice taken away or her feet cut off, or I could be the wily witch queen who got to tend her own garden of power, who got to take the voices, keep the feet, plant them, grow more feet. The message was clear: if I wanted love, I had to somehow figure out how to mermaid myself. This was truly terrifying to my little girl self, not least because I loved to talk all day long and then sometimes into the night. Perhaps due to my mother's generous recording of my childhood "poems," I fancied myself a writer at a young age. The notion of giving up what even then I saw as my voice, as my art, struck me as a tragedy.

I didn't understand why the mermaid couldn't find a prince who was willing to come live in the ocean with her, give up his feet, see a witch about acquiring a fish tail. That way she could keep her self and he could hear her sing underwater.

Singing is the little mermaid's art. In the film we see her missing her starring role in Sebastian's concert in the first scene. In the fairy tale she "sang more sweetly than them all. The whole court applauded her with hands and tails; and for a moment her heart felt quite gay, for she knew she had the loveliest voice of any on earth or in the sea. But she soon thought again of the world above her, for she could not forget the charming prince." She asks the witch, "But if you take away my voice...what is left for me?"

The witch answers, "Your beautiful form, your graceful walk, and your expressive eyes; surely with these you can enchain a man's heart." Even as a kid I could see how things were carved out for me: I would have to choose to be the artist or the work of art, and I wanted to be the artist so very badly. Chris Kraus nails my conundrum when she writes, "so what was Chris performing? At that moment she was a picture of the Serious Young Woman thrown off the rails, exposed, alone, androgynous and hovering onstage between the poet-men, presenters of ideas, and actress-women, presenters of themselves."

I simply couldn't wrap my youthful understanding around how the little mermaid's talent wasn't enough for her. She was the sweetest singer in the land. Her songs filled her with glee and caused the other mer-folk to clap with both their human and fish halves when they heard her. How could she still need a prince after that? How could she give it all up for him?

The Disney version of a desirable woman appeared to involve being a painting, beautiful and silent, so that men could imagine whatever they wanted upon you. "Taught from infancy that beauty is woman's sceptre," writes Mary Wollstonecraft (Mary Shelley's mother), "the mind shapes itself to the body, and roaming round its gilt cage, only seeks to adorn its prison." My best friend growing up was gorgeous and often silent, letting the boys read whatever they wanted from her, design her as their own most thrilling, mysterious, just out of reach fiction. I, on the other hand, always felt too big—big hands, big feet, big mouth, always eating too much and refusing to shrink to the correct proportions, talking so much, laughing so much, laying all my cards on the table. My view of what the males of my species wanted was of course limited and flat, but what can you expect of a girl brought up on fairy tales? More importantly, it seemed what I needed to do to be desirable was in direct contrast to what I needed to do to be an author. As any introductory writing teacher will tell you, it's all about finding your voice, so to agree to have it taken away is sort of step one in the what not to do department.

I wanted to turn and say to somebody in the theater, "but wouldn't any sane prince eventually get bored of a quiet mermaid who laughed soundlessly at all his jokes but never had a say in any matter?" While Ariel barters her art for romance, Ursula remains witchy and creative. As she sings her story-song in the film, she conjures images of what she's describing above her cauldron as all writers long to be able to do with their writing. She's capable of creative magic, of making something exist out of nothingness.

In contrast to the voiceless Ariel, Ursula's the first Disney villain to get her own song. Ursula belts out the phenomenal "Poor Unfortunate Souls" in that unforgettable husky Pat Carroll half-growl, shaking that lavish animated bosom in our faces, bursting the screen with the sheer fact of herself. In her wildness, she evades all attempts at definition.

72

Ursula doesn't even have quite enough tentacles to make her an official octopus hybrid (because that would have been too hard to animate), but this makes her even more so her own entity entirely. If the monster has long been read as the merger between human and animal or even multiple animals, Ursula isn't even a legible monster, and that's just how I liked her.

Even the bodies of the sea witch and the little mermaid were so different. I remember figuring that Ursula could probably stow the entire Ariel in her brassiere and nobody would be the wiser.

It was difficult to comprehend how that little mermaid, an almost invisible slip of a fish who hovers in the background while the sea witch sings, could ever ponder giving up still more of herself.

I started to see early how a certain kind of queering could liberate women somehow in creative ways. We can see the wildly divergent gender and sexuality messaging behind Ursula and Ariel in their animators' inspiration. For Ariel they looked to standard American male masturbation material, Alyssa Milano in *Who's the Boss,* and for Ursula they looked to Harris Milstead, a.k.a the drag performer Divine from such John Waters' films as the 1972 *Pink Flamingos.* It's only fitting since all Divine wanted as a young boy was to be a Disney Villain.

John Waters bestowed upon him his moniker, Divine, and his satirical tagline: "the most beautiful woman in the world, almost." This use of Divine, a drag performer who upends traditional notions of gender and sexuality, as a model fits the campy, powerful, genre-defying Ursula quite nicely. The choice also resonates with the fact that Anderson sent his *Little Mermaid* fairy tale to an unrequited male love interest. In keeping with this renegade gender and sexuality lineage, Ursula directly opposes Ariel, who serves as a love letter to heterosexual male desire.

I can still recall wondering what it would look like if Ariel and Ursula just forgot about the prince and married each other. I figured there would be a lot of bickering and breaking things, but at least nobody would have to give up either their tail or tale. Then again, Ursula would probably get bored of that relationship pretty fast.

With her sauciness and subversive subtext, Ursula has more panache in a single tentacle than Ariel, but I was assured it was Ariel in her practical nonexistence that was just the thing to turn boys' heads, and didn't I want to turn heads? I thought so, and yet I wanted to access Ursula's subversive power in my creative life, and the two desires seemed to be at odds with one another.

It struck me that both the creative and the monstrous lived beyond the borders of what is thinkable, and that was exactly where I wanted to go. I felt my writing to be a dark art brewing in some cauldron inside of me. I sensed that my creative force was buried deep down in my own private sea witch bower.

When I got bored in class, I would imagine alternative realities for that little mermaid in which she got to be more like the sea witch. In these waking dreams, Ariel sometimes took over Ursula's body, letting her fingers glide over her newfound expansiveness, palming a tentacle, singing all the while, making infinite potions.

I had a strange sense, though, that these two sea creations Ursula and Ariel were somehow more correlated than they first seemed. I later learned that mermaids have long been linked to the monstrous sirens, who more closely resemble the sea witch. The word mermaid is lexically like the Old English term *merewīf* or water-witch. In *The Odyssey,* another sea witch, Circe, tells Odysseus of the sirens, "There is a great heap of dead men's bones lying all around, with the flesh still rotting off them," and in the Little Mermaid fairy tale, the sea witch's lair is "built with the bones of shipwrecked human beings."

Sirens famously drew sailors to shipwreck, so that image of Ariel rescuing Prince Eric in the movie is a reversal of this. If the mermaid is the sea witch defanged, then the warning was this: if you don't watch your manners, if you don't mutilate yourself into the perfect mermaid, you will end up as the sea witch—alone and ultimately destroyed for the gender "safety" of our society, to ensure that our romance factory just keeps right on chugging. And so now I understand why successfully turning into a "woman" felt like losing my tail.

I remember when I was little, I would joyously lift my shirt to show my little boy friends that I was just like them, that we were the same, and back then we were. And then we weren't. It all felt like some outside force overtaking my body. As a teenager I felt like I was being pranked by some playful sprite who got her kicks by playing fast and loose with humans.

I suppose the mermaid monster appealed to me because who hasn't felt at least the littlest bit hybrid, part whatever this is and part something other, perhaps most vividly in adolescence when you truly are in the process of transforming from this to that.

Although softened to standard grade mean girls for the 1953 Disney movie, unlike Ariel, and in true sea witch fashion, the mermaids in J.M. Barrie's 1911 novel *Peter Pan* are truly dangerous. "A sound at once the most musical and the most melancholy in the world: the mermaids calling to the moon" haunts the book, and at one point, "a mermaid caught Wendy by the feet, and began pulling her softly into the water."

I was starting to see that I was in danger of acquiring some sort of Peter Pan syndrome myself if growing up meant I had to stop being the sea witch and instead become the boring, obedient little mermaid who can't feel complete without a man. And so I decided at the age of seven not to marry, to grow old and fat all alone in my fish bower, just writing all through the night, taking breaks only to howl at the moon. But then I woke up at 29, pregnant and married and writing a book. And then I woke up again at 34, pregnant again, with a three-year-old running around, and writing another book. It was this one.

Diablo Cody, a mother and screenwriter, who wrote the screenplay for a strange and beautiful movie about motherhood, with mermaid themes, *Tully,* says of the film, "The outward struggles of new moms have already been documented in films, TV shows and Tide commercials. It was the *inner* life of the new mother that I wanted to explore: the wild heart that still beats inside the docile cow." Like Marlo, the character in the movie (Charlize Theron), she had recently had number three, but unlike Marlo (and unlike the wife in Offill's *Dept of Speculation*), the English major who feels she's failed to do anything worthwhile with her degree, Cody had her art to rescue her. "Writing this script saved me. 'Tully' became my Tully, my helper, a glowing, soothing presence I could return to whenever I felt overwhelmed." This book was my Tully after I had my second child.

I had this sense that being a mother and an art monster were not only not mutually exclusive (although, as I've said, it requires a fight to the death), but they were potentially linked and could feed each other. Although having children certainly takes up time that I could be writing and emotionally drains me many days, I have also found having children to have inspired my writing. The baby can be the idea that breaks all prior ideas and makes way for a whole new mode of thought, the paradigm shift. Part of this is because they tend to find their way into my work in one way or another. Part of this is because I have chosen to see my literary and biological creation as feeding one another, as different ways of making. I am not saying this is an easy process. It's brutal many days. I'm often so moody I think it would be easier to get in there with construction equipment, and have that thing that looks like a claw remove all my mind matter, replace with nougat. Except that I'd probably eat it. But it's also heavenly to feel that I've created in two different dimensions—books and babies. It makes my life feel a little like science fiction, which, as other geeks will tell you, is always good.

77

There certainly is a tension that exists within the art monster concept between the role of writer and the role of mother, though, between reproductive/biological creativity and literary (or any other kind of) creativity, the competing needs of books and children. In response to this concern, I try to think of the "M" of "Mother" and the "W" of "Writer" as being flipped versions of one another, *Through the Looking-Glass* doppelgängers. But sometimes the stability of this understanding topples, and perhaps it was a fiction designed to contain my fear of the former devouring the latter all along. Some days the "M" seems to feast on the "W."

Mother and monster have long been linked in the collective consciousness. We can see this phenomenon's lighter and more humorous iterations, such as that episode of *Modern Family* wherein Manny's mother, Gloria, realizes she resembles the monster in her son's movie. The mother, the one who can give life is also often seen as the one who can potentially take it away. This is why many of the women accused of being witches were healers and midwives, for one thing. In Allen Ginsberg's *Kaddish*, for example, he sees his mother lying on the bed as though beckoning to him sexually and he contemplates with disgust and perhaps even a jagged, twisted desire visiting that, "Monster of the Beginning Womb" that is all maternal sexuality.

At the simplest level, Jason Reitman's *Tully* tells the tale of Marlo's (Charlize Theron) struggle with the arrival of her third child and consequent hiring of a night nanny named Tully.

When I got pregnant, I was suddenly multiple. I contained multitudes. A baby was growing in me, and suddenly I was aware of all sorts of other pregnant things: pregnant animals, pregnant thoughts. Even the reading I was doing for my dissertation informed me that the movie theater takes viewers back to an infantile state, how the screen was like a womb.

78

I wanted to know how I felt about motherhood as I went to sleep, so I posed the dream question like my father suggested. I dreamed I was supposed to get up and sing, but I explained to the person organizing the event: "everyone wants me to sing, but I've never heard the song." So my dad said that since I had that dream I should sing to my unborn baby to get him to come out. So I sat on the toilet and shyly crooned to him in my not so great voice, which was more likely to keep him in there indefinitely. Who in their right mind would come rushing towards a world that contained such a sound?

As Tully herself says, she's a way to "bridge the gap," but not in the way we thought. She's not merely a modern-day Mary Poppins there to ease the transition that is the new baby. "Tully" turns out to be Marlo's maiden name, the part of herself she shed when she became married and a mother—and perhaps three times to become a mother of three—that she has resurrected to survive the new baby. The word "maiden" recalls "maiden" journeys, or firsts, and, ironically enough, virginity—the opposite of where Marlo now finds herself, living in the land of lunch boxes and Legos.

And so Marlo conjures this enchanted Tully, who's simultaneously a mother, friend, sister, lover, and the wild and free part of herself that she has lost to domesticity. Right after Marlo's brother suggests she get a night nanny, she starts inventing her own Tully, her own "glowing, soothing presence [she can] return to whenever [she feels] overwhelmed," and starts having visions of mermaids. She's talking to her husband, and he senses he's lost her for a second the first time it happens. Right before her water breaks, it happens again. The next time she sees this mermaid is right before her new night nanny, Tully, gives her the baby to feed. Looking back, we see that the whole scene was a vision. The next time we see the mermaid she's rescuing a Marlo who's drunkenly driven herself into a body of water. Like the siren's song, new motherhood can also make you want to go jump in a lake. Just ask Marlo.

79

In keeping with Cody's desire to tell the story of "the wild heart that still beats inside the docile cow" of the mother, although it's easy to forget her connection to her fatal Siren ancestors, the mermaid is a monster. What defines both the mermaid and the monster is their undomesticated, boundary-breaking hybridity. A baby is also a hybrid, a mixture of the woman and man's genetic matter, all those sewn together stories of who they are and who they hope the baby will be.

One day this summer, I took my son to Coney Island so he could ride the little kid rollercoaster, the Sea Serpent, over and over and swim in the ocean. He used to do this thing where it looks like he's humping the floor, but when he did it in the water, I realized he'd been trying to swim on the ground all along. He was shivering but couldn't be coaxed out. He kept holding his little purple hands up to the waves like he was a wizard conjuring them. He kept flapping his imaginary tail and trying to tell me what the ocean meant to him. Finally, he turned to me, splashed water in my face, and said, "mama, I'm sea monster," and I said, "so am I."

And no wonder Marlo's overwhelmed enough to hallucinate savior mermaids. She doesn't only have the new baby, Mia. She also has an older daughter, Sarah, and the middle son, Jonah—a child whom various specialists can only describe as "atypical," which is where I found myself at the time. I picked my own son up each day hoping he got two checks so I could get him ice cream, that he hadn't sucked on Sammy's admittedly delicious-looking hair.

80

Cody wanted to write of the mother's inner life, and the sound of the mermaid's dwelling in Marlo's imaginings recalls a womb. Not everybody will recognize this, except maybe those who bought the app that's supposed to sound like a womb and therefore comfort the colicky child—or maybe just a child who will turn out to swim outside the waters of definability, with that mermaid.

The tricky thing is, if she's swimming in a womb, the mermaid is also the baby, the flapping fetus. Add to this the fact that this Tully/mermaid represents Marlo's younger, maiden self, and it starts to seem like Marlo's able to swim around in her own womb in these visions. Perhaps more precisely, she's able in this fantastic landscape to splash around in her own brain matter like a fish, in the lost but still present somehow, somewhere, caverns of who she once was.

It's not merely the gorgeousness of the mermaid's song that makes it so deadly. It's also otherworldly in a way that deranges the senses, a thought beyond thought, beauty that pushes human sensory powers beyond their own limits and therefore explodes them.

Some stories hold that mermaids are but love-struck lass-es, wanting to bring their human paramours to their home in the sea, without considering their lack of gills. This reminds me of motherhood in a strange way. You get to know your baby while s/he's underwater, living in *your* water, in fact. Later, s/he's a fish out of water that you then need to teach to walk. Mother and child have lived together in this ecstatic, safe, underwater oneness and then they are two, and both must find their land legs, so to speak.

In this sense, Tully (the nanny who is really a part of Marlo herself, and a link to both Mia's beginnings and even Marlo's own) embodies the strange, almost possessed, maternal experience of two beings in one body. No scene dramatizes this better than the one where Tully and Marlo have a threesome with Marlo's husband.

Hans Christian Anderson claims the mermaid's song is actually a form of compassion—a heavenly sound meant to comfort drowning men. This applies to motherhood and to *Tully*. Tully is the mermaid song meant to soothe Marlo (and Cody), who is drowning in new motherhood. Of course, in the film, Tully is also the meaner kind of mermaid song, which causes Marlo to drunkenly drive her car into a lake and almost drown herself. Although she does imagine a Tully-like mermaid swimming to save her, and she survives, which is perhaps yet another way that Tully is her savior mermaid.

What gives the movie nuance is how it doesn't only focus on what you lose in motherhood or how it's mindbogglingly hard. The film opens and closes on Marlo brushing her son. For those of you whose kids don't have "sensory issues," you may not know what this means. The idea is that your child's hypersensitive to touch (they either seek it out or avoid it) and therefore need to be brushed like a horse. When I first heard about the "problem" of my son's sensory issues, it saddened me that the joy he took in touching things, what I think of as his poet's nature, was being pathologized, but I also understood that he couldn't be licking the school desks. He is now older, still very creative, but no longer does this. Sometimes I wish he did. Some days I must hold myself back from licking desks so to speak, from wanting to love the world too hard, from wishing I could swim around inside my son as he once swam around inside me. But, see, life isn't built this way.

Marlo brushes his whole body. The film captures this intimate moment, how the light hits them as she does it, how she's physically close to him in a way she doesn't always get to be. We see everything about the surreal, sweet, wrenching journey that is motherhood in this scene. She looks exhausted, but like she now knows all sides of life—its storms and rainbows. This scene bookends the film, a kind of arrival and departure. Certain Old English tales make mermaids out to be signs of things to come, both capable of causing storms and spotting them. As Marlo brushes her son, she looks serene in this paradoxical way some mothers have that comes from knowing there will be storms, but she will just be there, brushing and brushing.

I'll never forget when that guy in college actually quoted Nietzsche while we were kissing: the perils of a liberal arts education. Before that we were fogging up windows, tapping out code on their panes. Believing himself, I guess, to be a creature of myth with a hint of both the minotaur and his prison maze, he whispered Nietzsche in my ear: "Be wise, Ariadne, you have small ears, you have my ears: let a wise word slip into them: Must one first not hate oneself, if one is to love oneself? I am your labyrinth." Needless to say, I never hooked up with him again.

Trouble was I didn't want to hate myself. I also didn't want to be Ariadne in our little drama. I preferred Theseus, Daedalus, the Minotaur, Asterion; I wanted to be the hero, the architect, or the monster but not the monster's sister who sold him out and was loved for one shining minute and then abandoned on an island.

But they tricked us with that Ariadne labyrinth business all along; it's not that they only hate and look down upon women's writing, although there's some of that I'm sure, but they need us to think that, so we don't see it coming when they steal it and pretend it was theirs all along. Ariadne led him, she told the yarn and then she was abandoned on that island or wherever.

I'm not sure when I became intrigued by the labyrinth, that real world counterpart to our inner space, external corollary to the thrilling but baffling inner tangle within us. Maybe it was when my friend Daniella and I discovered that mind-boggling book *House of Leaves* in the college bookstore about this photojournalist who moves into a house only to find that it's bigger on the inside than on the outside. He calls his twin brother to help him understand this home that's sprouting labyrinths suddenly. Danielewski includes reams of footnotes from fake critics, and now I wake to find myself a scholar, trying to make truth claims like all his phony theorists. I'm even here trying to do this with monsters.

Sometimes my dissertation and academic life feels like an exercise in gracefully manipulated bullshit—or is that just life? Impostor syndrome. There was that weird moment when I was in my third year of my PhD program, and I realized I didn't know how to spell exhilarated or diarrhea without looking them up.

Or maybe I became obsessed with labyrinths when I started taking philosophy classes in college and saw what this structure has meant to thinkers over time. Or maybe it was when I realized at whatever age it was that I had a mind, and then tried to use it to study that very same mind and became self-referential.

85

Perhaps philosophers link labyrinths to thought structures because of this eerie sense we have that we inhabit something that seems patternless but if we could only rise above ourselves and take a look, we'd suddenly get it.

Ariadne's thread, then, becomes our attempt to comprehend this labyrinth of consciousness we find ourselves wandering. And Ariadne, as the one who gets it, becomes the philosopher/artist/writer spinning her "thread"—not Theseus who merely steals it for his own heroics and then abandons her on an island.

What would thought's labyrinth even look like? This all begs the question: if our inner questioning chaos is a labyrinth, who built it?

Ovid describes Daedalus not only as architect but as artist capable of imbuing stone with uncertainty. It's hard to imagine a more marvelous endgame for art. Daedalus uses this gift to enclose the monster.

Another reason the labyrinth fascinates me is because of the monster at its center, at the center of us all. Remember that the minotaur is an unwanted child, the unacceptable offspring of our own selves, our own minds. But this is the part that for a writer is the most crucial to seek out.

It often feels to me that the monster chase scene is reversed: as a writer, I don't run from the monster but towards it, beg it to haunt my labyrinth. The monster is the story, the inspiration, the beating heart of narrative.

Walter Benjamin treated the city as labyrinth navigated by the flaneur which, in my model, would place the monster at the center of the city: the reward for our literal and intellectual wanderings.

The monster is not a deterrent; it's the whole point, the much-desired outcome of the hero/ine's journey that is writing. The writer/artist/philosopher is our guide not only to the labyrinth but, most critically, to the monster. The writer is the one who navigates the labyrinth, encounters the monster, and lives to tell about it.

According to its dictionary definition, a flâneur is little more than a loiterer, but to thinkers such as Walter Benjamin and Charles Baudelaire this figure plays the role of a city's cultural camera. But what does it mean to do what Virginia Woolf calls "street haunting"?

In "The Painter of Modern Life," Baudelaire's comparison of the flâneur's crowd to a fish's water has always stood out to me since we all know a fish will die without that particular fluid. This statement assigns life or death stakes to the art of taking in the city scene, and that's just how I like it.

I also like the joining together of one's passion and one's profession. I like even more when that profession involves merging with the urban spectacle to such an extent that you become a single skin. Baudelaire seems to say, if this creeps you out, you may not be flâneur material.

87

What does it mean to make your home in the jostle of the "fugitive and the infinite"? I suppose it means to inhabit that which is at once fleeting, even vaguely menacing, and also everlasting.

As an adjective, fugitive, too, means fleeting, but as a noun it's someone who must flee due to persecution. I imagine here that Baudelaire's flâneur inhabits some mixture of these two definitions: living evanescence and fleeing any life that doesn't prioritize ardent cultural spectatorship.

Baudelaire's description of the flâneur is full of contradiction, or at least the play of paradox. In his view, to be a flâneur you must be outside the house, out in the city, eating culture. But this stalking of the exterior must be so native that it becomes your only real home.

There's a relationship to the crowd here that's at once distant and intimate. You must remain hidden from the people of the city, but they also become your family. And to love them is to love electricity itself. In Baudelaire's rendition, you are the kaleidoscope that grew a philosophically inclined brain that recreates the details of all it captures and recasts.

Benjamin's take on the flâneur, a "werewolf roaming restlessly in the social wilderness," is as fervid as Baudelaire's but also contains a warning; this urban detective and delighter is also the perfect victim of the city's less savory offerings: capitalism and alienation.

Another disturbing aspect of flânerie is the degree to which it has been the province of men—an issue Lauren Elkin takes up beautifully in her book *Flâneuse*. Nevertheless, I live to walk my city. Let's just say that, even though this role wasn't readily offered up to me as a woman, I took it.

I often compose my writing as I stroll. This sense that my eyes are cameras, that what goes in is image and what comes out is writing has long been with me. As I walk, I insert a frame on what I'm looking at, and the whole city becomes edited, through this peculiar sort of attention, into art.

I often think how far from the original notion of the flâneur I am as I push two squawking kids in a double stroller along Greenwood Cemetery on the way to school. This makes me embrace the identity all the more. And so here I am, the "werewolf roaming restlessly in the social wilderness" . . . with a double stroller.

88

While writing my novel *Ghosts of America*, about a male author haunted by the women he has misrepresented in his career—Jackie Kennedy, among them–I immersed myself in U.S. history, gender issues, and the politics of being a first lady. I sent in my final edits and vowed to take a vacation from these topics, but then I relaxed by reading…four novels about first ladies: Curtis Sittenfeld's *American Wife* on Laura Bush and *Rodham* in which she imagines Hillary never married Bill, Ann Beattie's *Mrs. Nixon,* and Amy Bloom's *White Houses* on Eleanor Roosevelt. Each of which examine the struggle to move out of the domestic sphere and into the public arena, as a first lady or otherwise.

In these books, as in life, these first ladies become the battlefield for warring ideas about a woman's role in the home and outside of it, especially when they are mothers. In her memoir, *Becoming,* Michelle Obama reflects on how she longed to live "with the hat-tossing, independent-career-woman zest of Mary Tyler Moore," but ended up instead inhabiting the "self-sacrificing, seemingly bland normalcy of being a wife and a mother." As for me, if I get one more targeted ad for Mother's Day gifts that places women in the kitchen or nursery, my head will explode. Where are my targeted ads for rugged traveling tools for my next big adventure?

After reading up on Jackie while researching my novel, I wished she could speak back to the (mostly) men who have shaped her story over the decades. The very role of the First Lady is ancillary: she is the woman behind the man, the one who plans Christmas decorations while her husband runs the country. In this sense, the first lady dramatizes the struggle of the average woman to step out from behind the men in her life. I was particularly struck by the parts of the Jackie biographies that showed her trying to balance motherhood, first ladyhood, and any ambitions of her own; her excitement when she thought President Lyndon B. Johnson might make her U.S. ambassador to Mexico.

While reading about these first ladies' struggles to establish themselves as something more than accessories, I recalled the history of my own art form: the many men tasked with writing this nation into being with their so-called "Great American Novels," and how few women were on that list. While I was supposed to be writing my novel, I would Zombie-scroll, with two squirming kids on my lap, through articles about how, if women want to write Great American Novels they shouldn't have children or, if they absolutely must procreate, they should just have one. As a tongue-in-cheek response to this, I subtitled *Ghosts of America*, a "Great American Novel."

Around this time, I made the chilling realization that what a woman creates with her body (i.e., kids) is often set forth as the very reason she can't create anything outside of it. In Curtis Sittenfeld's *American Wife*, Alice (the Laura Bush character) muses on how the George Bush character's obsession with his legacy is so masculine. She concludes that you don't hear women freaking out about their legacies. When she mentions this to her husband, he says it's because women are the ones making babies, as though that's the sole endgame of their ambition. Maybe I'm not supposed to admit this here but, despite the baby butt wiping or perhaps even more so because of it, I did freak out about my legacy. As absurd as it may sound, I obsessively pictured clawing my way out of a mountain of diapers to one day ascend some illusory literary peak.

In Sittenfeld's *Rodham*, the title character, who gets to inhabit a speculative universe where she wields the kind of power real-life Hillary never got to, is notably childless. And there I was, notably covered in children but still seeking my own kind of power, living the dumpster fire that is the modern mom "trying to have it all." I was attempting to keep my new job as an assistant professor and writing program director during a pandemic, with no childcare, prying filthy things from my children's cute little fingers, while writing a novel chronicling the challenges women face when it comes to having anything, much less "it all."

When the real-life Hillary was asked about her job as a successful lawyer, she replied, "I suppose I could have stayed home and baked cookies and had teas, but what I decided to do was to fulfill my profession." Of course, the public flayed her for this. Afterwards, the *Washington Post* asked: "Hillary Clinton, Trying to Have it All; Lawyer, Author, Activist, Strategist, Mother, Political Wife … and Now, Political Problem?" But, of course, the real political problem wasn't merely Hillary's cookie comment; it was the tension between the identities in the *WaPo* headline. When Hillary became a "problem," she had to transition from talking policy to a bake-off with Barbara Bush, her policy negotiations reduced to the merits of cookie recipes with shortening (Hillary) versus without (Barbara).

In *Mrs. Nixon*, Ann Beattie, too, wrestles with the

limited sphere of the first lady. She touches on the criticism Hillary received for her cookie comment and the backlash that followed Michelle Obama's claim that she wasn't always proud of her country. Beattie considers how women are taught to, as Sittenfeld says, live lives that exist in opposition to themselves, simultaneously making and unmaking themselves daily. Beattie even features a scene where Hillary nervously bakes cookies with a more cookie-competent Pat Nixon.

As Amy Bloom puts it in *White Houses,* Eleanor Roosevelt "was a Great Lady and what man in Christ's name wanted to be married to that?" If you think the stigma surrounding female ambition is also a thing of the past, just Google, "Hillary Clinton literal imbiber of children's blood," and you'll see how she has been portrayed for daring to ascend a political ladder thought to be the provenance of men.

I'm not sure where all this leaves me with my whole fantasy of battling a battalion of diapers to climb some literary peak, but considering the politics of being a first lady alongside my own plight certainly highlighted for me the simultaneous pressure and impossibility for women to "have it all."

But what do we have instead? A hopeful, creative chaos that we determinedly face every day, and maybe even our own speculative *Rodhame*sque universes where we live more vital parallel lives. And perhaps, through our own radical innovations, we just might even step into these lives one day. In the meantime, I'll just be here in my "study," typing this in gym socks and cat pajaamas, pockets full of candy wrappers, my son informing me that I just misspelled "pajamas," as I seek to build my legacy out of popsicle sticks.

Acknowledgments

Earlier versions of some of this material have appeared in *The Kenyon Review, Huffington Post, Elle, Epiphany,* and *Creative Nonfiction.* Thanks so much to T. Thilleman and Aurelia at Spuyten Duyvil for working so hard to make this book a reality and to Robin Tewes for letting me use her amazing cover art. Thanks to my family and friends for all the love and support. And thanks to all you Art Monsters out there. I see you.

CAROLINE HAGOOD is Assistant Professor of Literature, Writing and Publishing and Director of Undergraduate Writing at St. Francis College in Brooklyn. She is the author of two poetry books, *Lunatic Speaks* and *Making Maxine's Baby*, a book-length essay, *Ways of Looking at a Woman*, and a novel, *Ghosts of America*.

Made in the USA
Middletown, DE
30 October 2022

13739061R00097